The James Club
and
the Original A.A. Program's
Absolute Essentials

Dick B.'s Reference Titles on Alcoholics Anonymous History Paradise Research Publications, Inc., Publisher;
Good Book Publishing Company, Distributor P.O. Box 837, Kihei, HI 96753-0837
Phone/Fax: (808) 874 4876; Email: dickb@dickb.com; URL: http://www.dickb.com/index.shtml
Publisher's November 1, 2005 List of Titles by Author Dick B.; All list prices: Effective November 1, 2005

Anne Smith's Journal, 1933-1939, 3rd ed.; 1998; 6 x 9; 180 pp.; $16.95

By the Power of God: A Guide to Early A.A. Groups & Forming Similar Groups Today; 2000, 6 x 9; 260 pp., $16.95

Cured!: Proven Help for Alcoholics and Addicts; 2003, 6 x 9; 182 pp., $17.95

Dr. Bob and His Library, 3rd ed.; 1998; 6 x 9; 156 pp.; $15.95

God and Alcoholism: Our Growing Opportunity in the 21st Century; 2002; 6 x 9; 190 pp.; $17.95

Good Morning!: Quiet Time, Morning Watch, Meditation, and Early A.A.; 2d ed.; 1998; 6 x 9; 154 pp.; $16.95

Henrietta B. Seiberling: Ohio's Lady with a Cause, Rev. ed.; 2004; 46 pp.; 8 ½ x 11; spiral bound, $15.95

Making Known The Biblical History and Roots of Alcoholics Anonymous: An Eleven-Year Research, Writing, Publishing and Fact Dissemination Project, 2001, 160 pp., spiral bound, $24.95

New Light on Alcoholism: God, Sam Shoemaker, and A.A.; 2d ed.; 1999; 6 x 9; 672 pp.; $24.95

The Akron Genesis of Alcoholics Anonymous, 2d ed.; 1998; 6 x 9; 400 pp.; $17.95

The Books Early AAs Read for Spiritual Growth, 7th ed.; 1998; 6 x 9; 126 pp.; $15.95

The First Nationwide A.A. History Conference - Comments of Dick B., 2003, 8 ½ x 11, 79 pp., spiral bound, $17.95

The Golden Text of A.A.: God, the Pioneers, and Real Spirituality; 1999; 6 x 9; 76 pp.; $14.95

The Good Book and The Big Book: A.A.'s Roots in the Bible; 2d ed.; 1997; 6 x 9; 264 pp.; $17.95

The James Club: The Original A.A. Program's Absolute Essentials, 3rd ed., 2005; 6 x 9; $17.95

The Oxford Group & Alcoholics Anonymous, 2d ed.; 1998; 6 x 9; 432 pp.; $17.95

That Amazing Grace (Clarence & Grace S.); 1996; 6 x 9; 160 pp.; $16.95

Turning Point: A History of Early A.A.'s Spiritual Roots and Successes; 1997; 6 x 9; 776 pp.; $29.95

Twelve Steps for You: Let Our Creator, A.A. History, and the Big Book Be Your Guide; 2003; 8 ½ x 11; spiral bound; 45; pp. $17.95

Utilizing Early A.A.'s Spiritual Roots for Recovery Today; Rev. ed.; 1999; 6 x 9; 106 pp., $14.95

When Early AA s Were Cured and Why; 2003; 8 ½ x 11; spiral bound; 114 pp.; $17.95

Why Early A.A. Succeeded: The Good Book in Alcoholics Anonymous Yesterday and Today (a Bible Study Primer), 2001; 6 x 9; 340 pp., $17.95

Available through other distributors

Hope: The Story of Geraldine O. Delaney, 2d ed. NJ: Alina Lodge

Our Faith Community A.A. Legacy (Dick B., ed and compiler). FL: Came to Believe Publications

Courage to Change (with Bill Pittman). MN: Hazelden

Women Pioneers of AA (Dick B., contributor). MN: Hazelden

The James Club
and
the Original A.A. Program's
Absolute Essentials

Dick B.

Paradise Research Publications, Inc.
P.O. Box 837, Kihei, HI 96753-0837

Paradise Research Publications, Inc.
P.O. Box 837
Kihei, HI 96753-0837
(808) 874-4876
Email: dickb@dickb.com
URL: http://www.dickb.com/index.shtml

This Paradise Research Publications Edition is published by arrangement with Good Book Publishing Company, PO Box 837, Kihei, HI: 96753-0837

The publication of this volume does not imply affiliation with, nor approval or endorsement from Alcoholics Anonymous World Services, Inc. The views expressed herein are solely those of the author. A.A. is a program of recovery from alcoholism–use of the Twelve Steps in connection with programs and activities which are patterned after A.A. but which address other problems, does not imply otherwise.

Note: All Bible verses quoted in this book, unless otherwise noted, are from the Authorized (or "King James") Version. The letters "KJV" are used when necessary to distinguish it from other versions.

ISBN: 1-885803-99-0

To Rev. Ken Burns, who gently has propelled me toward continuing Bible study and contributed an immense amount of research material since 1979, and before.

Contents

Introduction

What's Here

If you would like to know exactly what early A.A. pioneers considered absolutely essential to their original spiritual program of recovery, then this is the book for you. I also believe it is top reading if you want to know the fundamentals that propelled A.A. to its astonishing successes and cures in its first decade of existence.

And such a basic study is long overdue. It appears never to have been done, and certainly not since A.A. co-founder Dr. Bob's death. Its significance is underlined by what A.A. Co-founder Dr. Bob was still emphasizing at A.A.'s June 9 and 10, 1945 "Big Meeting," with an estimated attendance of 2,500, at the Cleveland Music Hall and Carter Hotel celebrating A.A.'s 10th anniversary. For, at that anniversary, the following specific remarks were recorded:

> **A.A. co-founder Dr. Bob commented that over the previous 10 years, he had averaged at least an hour's reading per day and "always returned to the simple teachings in the Sermon on the Mount, the Book of James, and the 13th chapter of First Corinthians in the Bible for his fundamentals"** (email from Arthur S. to Dick B., dated November 28, 2004, in which Arthur said the foregoing is an extract from the July, 1945 *Grapevine*; emphasis added).

Such continuing and repeated remarks by Dr. Bob about James, the Sermon, and Corinthians strongly suggested to me a title which would look directly and in detail at the very Bible verses AAs were reading and studying and show us all just what our pioneers borrowed from, the Book of James, the Sermon on the Mount (Matthew 5-7), and 1 Corinthians 13.

The Book of James is first in study priority: The Book of James comes first in our study for many reasons. First of all, it was the undisputed Bible favorite of early AAs. It comes first because they liked its contents so much they wanted to call their society the James Club—rather than Alcoholics Anonymous. It comes first because our Big Book has taken more ideas from the verses of James than from other parts of the Bible. It comes first because you'll recognize some direct Big Book quotes from James even though Bill Wilson never gave any recognition to their Bible source. James comes first because its phrase "faith without works is dead" became a launching pad for such well-known A.A. language as that in the verse itself, and the adaptations of it found in Bill Wilson's "Works Publishing Company;" in the Big Book sentence, "It works;" in the Big Book Chapter Five title, "How It works;" and perhaps even in the enthusiastic arm-shaking that ends most A.A. meetings—with a robust circle of members who recite the Lord's Prayer and follow it with the shout: "Keep coming back. It works." There is an additional reason for our James emphasis: James is probably the easiest of the three essential parts of the Good Book to read and understand. Despite all these important attributes, James is the book which had no specific accompanying commentary that the pioneers used—commentaries like the many on the Sermon on the Mount and Henry Drummond's *The Greatest Thing in the World* on 1 Corinthians 13.

The Sermon on the Mount: Next in order comes Jesus' Sermon on the Mount. You'll find it in Matthew chapters 5, 6, and 7. It's probably the best known part of the Bible today. It's probably been the subject of more popular religious writings than most parts of the Bible. Bill and Bob both said it contained the "underlying philosophy" of A.A. And, though most AAs probably don't know it, the Lord's Prayer—which they recite at the end of most of their meetings—is part of the Sermon. Moreover, there are some real fundamental Twelve Step ideas which have their basic origin in some of the verses in the Sermon.

1 Corinthians: Finally, there's the little chapter in 1 Corinthians. It's the Thirteenth Chapter. It became the focus of a great deal of Christian literature. It was the subject of Professor Henry Drummond's best-selling book *The Greatest Thing in the World*. Its real punch, as far as A.A. was concerned, lies in just two or three of its verses which defined the nine "ingredients" of love, as Henry Drummond articulated them. And the Drummond book was possibly the book most recommended and circulated by Dr. Bob to early AAs and their families. You'll see lots more when you get into it here.

What's Elsewhere

I like to beef up our historical material with supplements in the Appendices. And you will find these supplements in the following appendices.

Appendix 1—The Specifics of our Pioneer Program: I think you'll want to review exactly what the early A.A. program was like. I've told the details many times elsewhere. But Appendix One will give you a brief, specific, and useful description.

Appendix 2—The Little-known Akron roots in United Christian Endeavor: I think you and lots of others will be surprised to see how much of our simple, early A.A. Christian program came from the principles and practices of the United Christian Endeavor Society in which Dr. Bob was an active participant as a youngster in his North St. Johnsbury Congregational Church. Appendix Two will provide you with the opportunity to compare the Christian Endeavor's confession of Christ, conversion meetings, prayer meetings, Bible-study meetings, Quiet Hour, fellowship, witness, and emphasis on love and service with the almost completely parallel elements of pioneer A.A.'s Akron Number One—the Christian Fellowship that developed and tested our original A.A. program.

Appendix 3—The Totally Divergent Two Roots of A.A.: Appendix Three will show you the two completely different origins of A.A.

The first root had its beginnings in Dr. Bob's participation in St. Johnsbury's North Congregational Church and its youth organization—Christian Endeavor; and it continued via Bob's life-long religious memberships and practices. It moved forward through Henrietta Seiberling's successful efforts to bring prayer and reliance on the Creator to the alcoholism recovery scene. And then it took more organized form in the "old fashioned prayer meetings" of the first forty pioneers— whose meetings exemplified their unity of purpose. It culminated in the work that brought astonishing successes and cures to the pioneer A.A. scene in Akron. It was thoroughly based on basic ideas taken from the Bible.

The second root was of an entirely different character. Unfortunately, most AAs don't know that. And most think that the Akron and New York activities were very similar because of their common Oxford Group link. They just don't know how Akron got its beginnings in United Christian Endeavor, while, the New York ideas began with Dr. Jung's "conversion" prescription to Rowland Hazard in Switzerland. From there, it was fashioned by Rowland's Oxford Group membership, by Rowland's sharing with Ebby Thacher, by Thacher's sharing with Bill Wilson, and by Wilson's acceptance of Christ at the altar of Calvary Rescue Mission. The weaving thread continued at Towns Hospital in New York via Bill Wilson's validation of his supposed "conversion experience" on his reading of Professor William James' book on a variety of religious experiences. Four years after Akron's simple program had been developed, New York took its basic life-changing ideas from the Oxford Group, the teachings of Rev. Sam Shoemaker, and the journal kept by Dr. Bob's wife. Wilson's New York ideas were then materially expanded by incorporating the medical views of Dr. William D. Silkworth, the lay therapy ideas of Richard Peabody, the influx of the New Thought Movement writings, and even Wilson's apparent admiration and utilization of New Age language.

Appendix 4—An Historical Analysis of the all-important Book of James. Appendix Four contains a complete study of the origins of the Book of James itself. It deals with James, the Lord's brother; the probable author of the Book of James; the canon difficulties involved in recognizing the book, and its importance as a source of healing ministries, similar to some conducted in early A.A. itself.

Appendix 5—A Simple Review of the Biblical Records about Yahweh, the one living and true God, our Creator and the distinction A.A. Pioneers drew between Almighty God and the later "nonsense gods of recovery."

Much of the angry outcries in today's Twelve Step Fellowships could have been and could be avoided by the dissemination of some solid historical facts about Yahweh, the one living and true God, whom A.A. founders appropriately called their Creator, Maker, Father of Lights, and Heavenly Father. This because it seemed to have taken at least a decade after A.A.'s founding before New Age substitutes began flooding America and A.A. itself. Phrases like "higher power," "Spirit of the Universe," and other New Age jargon were able—because of the dearth of history about A.A.'s real roots in the Bible and real sought-after relationship with Him—to inject New Age "spirituality" in the form of compromise and illusory substitutes for the Creator Yahweh, the living God of Roman Catholics, Protestants, and Jews alike. This appendix will enable you, if you choose, to know the real God from the idolatrous present-day gods that are called light-bulbs, radiators, chairs, Santa Claus, and all the rest. These idols are confounding clergy, recovering people, and scholars alike.

Now, let's return to our study of the three parts of the Bible that Dr. Bob mentioned so often and that he and A.A. old-timers considered to be the absolute essentials of early A.A.'s spiritual recovery program.

Part One:

A.A.'s Book of James

The Favorite of Three Parts of the Bible Early AAs Considered Essential

Early, Widespread A.A. Enthusiasm for the Book of James

What the Founders Said:

Bill Wilson had gotten sober in New York at Towns Hospital in late 1934. He went to Akron on a business deal, and met Dr. Bob Smith at Henrietta Seiberling's Gate House. Shortly thereafter, at Anne Smith's suggestion, Bill moved in with the Smiths. Though not particularly accurate in its characterization of the daily Bible readings, one official A.A. history says:

> Bill now joined Bob and Anne in the Oxford Group practice of having morning guidance sessions together, with Anne reading from the Bible [Note: Oxford Group 'guidance' did often involve reading from the Bible, but the Smith-Wilson Bible studies were inappropriately called 'guidance' sessions; the studies were directed at the Bible itself, at prayer, at literature, and at such revelation from their Heavenly Father as they chose to seek]

[The A.A. account continues:]. "Reading. . . from her chair in the corner, she would softly conclude, >Faith without works is dead.' "As Dr. Bob described it, they were 'convinced that the answer to our problems was in the Good Book. To some of us older ones, the parts that we found absolutely essential were the Sermon on the Mount [Matthew, Chapters 5-7], the 13th chapter of First Corinthians, and the Book of James**. The Book of James was considered so important, in fact, that some early members even suggested The James Club as a name for the Fellowship'."** (See *Pass It On*. NY: Alcoholics Anonymous World Services, Inc., 1984, p. 147; emphasis added)**.**

Published four years earlier, and written by a different author, another A.A. "Conference Approved" history tells the facts somewhat more accurately. Thus *DR. BOB and the Good Oldtimers* (NY: Alcoholics Anonymous World Services, Inc., 1980), states at p. 71:

"For the next three months [after Bill met Bob in May of 1935], I [Bill] lived with these two wonderful people," Bill said. "I shall always believe they gave me more than I ever brought them." Each morning, there was a devotion, he recalled. After a long silence, in which they awaited inspiration and guidance, Anne would read from the Bible. "James was our favorite," he said. "Reading from her chair in the corner, she would softly conclude, 'Faith without works is dead.' This was a favorite quotation of Anne's, much as **the Book of James was a favorite with early A.A.'s so much so that 'The James Club' was favored by some as a**

name for the Fellowship (emphasis added).

In his own history of early A.A., Bill Wilson wrote:

> And we could remember Anne as she sat in the corner by the fireplace, reading from the Bible the warning of James, that "faith without works is dead." (*Alcoholics Comes of Age*. NY: Alcoholics Anonymous World Services, Inc., 1967, p.7).

Historian Ernest Kurtz quoted **Wilson as saying, "We much favored the Apostle James"** (Ernest Kurtz, *Not-God*, Expanded ed. (MN: Hazelden, 1991, pp. 40, 320, n.11, emphasis added).

John R. was a well-known, long-lived Akron A.A. old-timer. And John specifically recalled as to these matters that much of the work on the writing of the Big Book "went on the Q.T." He said the average member wasn't aware of it. Then, as to the name Alcoholics Anonymous that was proposed for the Big Book, John R. tells us this in *DR. BOB*, *supra*, p. 213:

> "Take the name A.A., for instance," said John. "The people here in Akron didn't like it, and they were saying no. Wally G.—said, **'Hey, what's with this A.A. deal? We want to call it Saint James.'** But Doc knew all the time that they were going to call it A.A. . . . They had it that way before we knew it. Then it dawned on Wally that he was arguing against it and they had already named it. Boy, that used to make him sore! But he was a nice guy" (emphasis added).

Historian Bill Pittman wrote of an alleged "**Dr. Bob's Required Reading List"—something that Dr. Bob's daughter told me did not exist. However,** among his five named "required" items, Pittman placed first on his list "The Holy Bible, King James Version. The Sermon on the Mount, the Lord's Prayer, **The Book of James**, The 13th Chapter of First Corinthians" (Bill Pittman, *AA The Way It Began*. Seattle: Glen Abbey Books, 1988, p. 197; emphasis added).

In his last major address to AAs in 1948, **Dr. Bob said:**

> When we started in on Bill D. [A.A. Number Three], we had no Twelve Steps. ...But we were convinced that the **answer to our problems** was in the Good Book. To some of us older ones, the parts that we found **absolutely essential were** the Sermon on the Mount, the thirteenth chapter of First Corinthians**, and the Book of James**.... (*The Co-Founders of Alcoholics Anonymous. Biographical sketches their last major talks*. NY: Alcoholics Anonymous World Services, Inc., 1972, 1975, pp. 9-10; emphasis added).

In a pamphlet published by the Friday Forum Luncheon Club of the Akron A.A. Groups, the pamphlet's writer selected the following from a "lead" [talk] given by Dr. Bob in Youngstown, Ohio:

> Members of Alcoholics Anonymous begin the day with a prayer for strength and a short period of Bible reading**. They find the basic messages they need in** the Sermon on the Mount, in Corinthians **and the Book of James** (Dick B., *The Good Book and The Big Book: A.A.'s Roots in the Bible,* 2d ed, Kihei, HI: Paradise Research Publications, Inc., 1997, p 21; emphasis added).

A pamphlet published by "AA of Akron," and written at the request of Dr. Bob states:

> **There is the Bible that you haven't opened for years. Get acquainted with it. Read it with an open mind**. You will find things that will amaze you. You will be convinced that certain passages were written with you in mind. Read the Sermon on the Mount (Matthew V, VI, and VII). Read St. Paul's inspired essay on love (I Corinthians XIII). **Read the Book of James**. Read the Twenty-third and Ninety-first Psalms. **These readings are brief but so important** (Dick B., *The Good Book and The Big Book*, *supra*, p. 20; emphasis added).

Several others who have researched our history have also confirmed this early James emphasis

See Nan Robertson, *Getting Better Inside Alcoholics Anonymous*. (NY: Fawcett Crest, 1988), p. 47; Bill Pittman. *AA: The Way It Began*, *supra*, pp. 182-183, 197; Mitchell K., *How It Worked: The Story of Clarence H. Snyder* (Washingtonville, NY: AA Big Book Study Group, 1999), pp. 69, 103-104; Dick B., *That Amazing Grace: The Role of Clarence and Grace S. in Alcoholics Anonymous*. (San Rafael, CA: Paradise Research Publications, 1996), pp. 34-37, 71, 73-76; Dick B., *The Good Book and The Big Book*, *supra*, See the Foreword by Dr. Bob's son, Robert R. Smith; Charles Taylor Knippel. *Samuel M. Shoemaker's Theological Influence on William G. Wilson's Twelve Step Spiritual Program of Recovery*. (St. Louis: Ph. D. Dissertation Presented to the Faculty of the Graduate School of Saint Louis University, 1987); Wally P., *But For the Grace of God...*

(WV: The Bishop of Books, 1995), pp. 32, 39, 45, 205, 211-213, 225; *Women Pioneers in 12 Step Recovery* (MN: Hazelden, 1999), pp. 1-2, 11-16.

As we will discuss shortly, Nora Smith Holm's *The Runner's Bible: Spiritual Guidance for People on The Run* (Colorado: Acropolis Books, Publisher, 1998 Edition) was very popular in pioneer A.A. and used particularly by Dr. Bob .That devotional was filled with references to verses in James that became part and parcel of A.A. language and ideas. See pp.16, 46, 51, 73, 79, 81, 86-87, 95-98, 100-101, 106, 110, 121, 126-127, 139, 152, 181, 184, 186, 221, 230, 245-246. And I found virtually the same plethora of relevant James quotations in the four years of quarterlies published *by The Upper Room* between 1935 and 1939, and used daily by the pioneers. Bill Wilson's secretary Nell Wing has also written a good bit on the Bible study and emphasis in early A.A. There is plenty of further confirmation of the enthusiasm for the Bible (which early AAs called "The Good Book,") and the Book of James among those pioneer AAs. But the foregoing comments by the founders, and the research work of many should suffice to prove that you and I, if we want to know about A.A., need to know much more about the Book of James.

The Burial of A.A.'s Bible Roots and Particularly Its Book of James Root

If I were to characterize the demise of our complete history, our Bible roots, and the proof of cures in A.A., I would phrase the actual process as follows: First, ignore the Bible, Jesus, and the cures. Then ignore Quiet Time, Anne Smith, Rev. Sam Shoemaker, and the Christian literature they read. Then turn the spotlight in a completely different direction: Just focus on what was allegedly wrong with Frank Buchman and the Oxford Group. Tell AAs that Dr. Bob tried to rely on the Bible, church, prayer, and the Oxford Group, but got drunk. Tell AAs the original A.A. pioneers practically all died drunk. Tell them the key to A.A. effectiveness lies primarily in one drunk's sharing his experience, strength, and hope with another still-suffering drunk. Tell people A.A. is "spiritual, but not religious." Tell them "recovery" is not about a "conversion," but about a "spiritual awakening." Tell them that even if they have an "awakening," they will never be cured. Add that they can merely have an "awakening" by taking the 12 Steps. Tell them the "awakening" amounts only to a "personality change." Tell them that even their "awakening" can only offer a "daily reprieve" from the curse of alcoholism—never a cure or complete release like the pioneers described. And tell them they can believe in any "god" they invent or choose, or in no god, or in "Something," or in nothing at all. But never ever tell them that almost all the foregoing "real" recovery program ideas were never the program of early A.A. and are about ninety percent baloney.

If you think the foregoing statements are neither accurate nor typical, I can tell you, and document my statement, that every one of these falsehoods, distortions, and pieces of guesswork can be found in the fellowship, the writings, and the 'histories' that abound today.

Parenthetically, I can affirm that the first paragraph above does not describe the A.A. I joined, nor the A.A. in which I recovered and was cured; nor does it even faintly resemble the beliefs and practices of the pioneers or the guidelines they found in the Book of James. In fact, all these distortions seem more the product of confused, incomplete, irreligious histories and historians than what you find in our meetings, in our Fellowship, in our Big Book, or in our Twelve Steps. The repeated telling of these purported facts has done much to emasculate A.A. as I know it and knew about it as an energetically active member. Endless supposedly sincere "recovery" talk has spawned endless confused thinking and sharing. Often fleeing from death, insanity, or jail, we sick ones jump on what we hear and then undergo controversy and angry remarks when we finally wake up. There is an old A.A. adage: "Came. Came to. Came to believe." It used to refer to Yahweh. Today, AAs and others are urged to believe in whatever they want or in nothing at all. ***The gaps in historical approaches***: Now we go briefly to what I see as a totally inadequate and negative historical approach to A.A.

As stated, there is ample evidence that the program was developed in Akron. There is ample evidence that the program was Christian in character. There is ample evidence that, when Dr. Bob decided firmly to quit drinking and place his reliance on our "Heavenly Father" as revealed in the "Good Book," he got well. And that he immediately became the mentor and major advocate for the basic Bible ideas that produced the effective results in early A.A. There is ample evidence that the Bible was read in meetings, stressed, and used as the basic source for A.A. ideas. There is ample evidence that Akron A.A. was not Oxford Group A.A. certainly not of the variety with which Bill, Lois, Hank Parkhurst, Rev. Sam Shoemaker, Rev. Irving Harris, and the sparse in number Eastern AAs were involved. Where is this evidence among the ever-growing numbers of historical books about A.A. today?

My recent research has disclosed much evidence that most of the successful Akron Biblical ideas emerged from Dr. Bob's own religious reading, his continuing and substantial church membership, and his participation in Christian Endeavor in his youth. See Dick B., *When Early AAs Were Cured. And Why* (Kihei, HI: Paradise Research Publications, Inc., 2003), pp. 6-13. As to the Oxford Group, the Akron fellowship was, at most, what pioneer Oxford Group activist T. Henry Williams called it: "sort of a clandestine lodge of the Oxford Group" (*DR. BOB*, *supra*, p. 121). One pioneer called this unique Christian Fellowship "a regular old-fashioned prayer meeting (*DR. BOB*, *supra*, p. 101). Dr. Bob's son described it as an "old fashioned revival meeting." Dr. Bob's daughter told me that her dad called every meeting a "Christian Fellowship." And that is confirmed by A.A. historical accounts (See *DR. BOB*, *supra*, p. 118). No other Oxford Groups [other than the little handful of Oxford Groupers that met with the drunks at the T. Henry Williams home in Akron] were devoted to helping drunks via meetings, a fellowship, teaching, and prayer in the manner employed by Dr. Bob's Christian Fellowship.

The Missing Facts: The foregoing Akron historical material is just plain missing from almost every recent historical writing about A.A. Among these, there is little or no mention of the Bible. There is little or no mention of Quiet Time. There is little or no mention of Rev. Sam Shoemaker. There is little or no mention of Anne Ripley Smith and her major role in early A.A. as "Mother of A.A." (an affectionate title given her by Bill Wilson and many others in the Fellowship). There is much more *criticism* of the Oxford Group than there is an accurate description of its twenty-eight basic ideas and their enormous impact on Bill's Big Book and Twelve Steps. See Dick B., *The Oxford Group and Alcoholics Anonymous: A Design for Living That Works*, 2d ed. (Kihei, HI: Paradise Research Publications, Inc., 1998). There is virtually no discussion of the content and impact of the Christian devotionals *The Upper Room*, *My Utmost for His Highest*, *The Imitation of Christ*, *The Greatest Thing in the World*, *The Runner's Bible*, and others that were daily fare in early A.A. There is seldom any mention of the Christian books early AAs read usually just a focus on the books of Professor William James (a non-Christian) and Emmet Fox (a Christian of the "New Thought Movement" variety). By contrast, writers of A.A. history have made little or no mention of the voluminous writings of Rev. Sam Shoemaker, Glenn Clark, Oswald Chambers, E. Stanley Jones, Harry Emerson Fosdick, Toyohiko Kagawa, and Oxford Group authors who were widely read for spiritual growth in early A.A. In fact, Dr. Bob circulated those materials, kept a journal of the people to whom the books were loaned, required their return, and then asked questions of the readers as to what they read and what they had discovered from their reading.

Clearly missing also is mention of Jesus Christ. There is no mention of the gift of the Holy Spirit. And you will search high and low for any mention of the much favored Book of James as a key to the solution to their problems and to cure by the power of God. Historian Ernest Kurtz hit the nail on the head:

> Yet A.A.'s total omission of "Jesus," its toning down of even "God" to a "Higher Power" which could be the group itself, and its changing of the verbal first message into hopeless helplessness rather than salvation. . . were profound changes" (Kurtz, *Not-God*, *supra*, p. 50).

Kurtz is dead right about the revision of, and changes, in A.A. But he certainly cannot speak, as he seems to do, for A.A.—or for me—as to what "A.A." is or does. Nor as to what "A.A." omitted, toned down, or changed. His views are much colored by his persistent and consistent claim that A. A. is about "not-god-ness." See Kurtz, *supra*, pp.150, 160, 185, 206-07, 218-19. This alleged wedding between A.A.'s Christian Fellowship and Kurtz's "not-god-ness" is just plain fiction. Regrettably, his views are echoed by many historians today, but they are examples of the very "rigidity" and "discipline" which perhaps emanate from Kurtz's training and former status as a Roman Catholic priest. But, whatever Kurtz and even some AAs may think they find in A.A. today, there is certainly no agreed or documented thought control ex cathedra that justifies stating that A.A. omitted Jesus, toned down God, and or transformed salvation to helplessness. That kind of revisionist thinking just has no universal acceptance. Nor does it make sense—salvation to helplessness? Come on. Think. Think. Think. Moreover, such rigidity and doctrinal contentions have been severely questioned by many including two that are (happily for the purposes of argumentation and refutation) quoted in Kurtz's Not-god treatise.

Thus a 1983 A.A. Conference keynote speaker (a Canadian, and trustee) is quoted as saying:

> . . . there appears to be developing within our Society a rigidity, a perceived need for law and order, a determination to enforce the Traditions to the letter, without any elasticity. If that attitude became widespread, the Fellowship could not function (Kurtz, *supra*, p 266).

Three years later, retiring G.S.O. senior advisor Bob P, a director and trustee for six years and its general manager for a decade said:

> If you were to ask me what is the greatest danger facing A.A. today, I would have to answer the growing *rigidity* the increasing demand for absolute answers to nit-picking questions, pressure for GSO to "enforce" our Traditions, screening alcoholics at closed meetings; prohibiting non-Conference approved literature, i.e. "banning books;" laying more and more rules on groups. . . (Kurtz, *supra*, pp.266-67).

Corroborating ex-trusted servant Bob P.'s comments are interesting pieces of history included by Historian Mitchell K. in his title *How It Worked: The Story of Clarence H. Snyder and the Early Days of Alcoholics Anonymous in Cleveland, Ohio.* (NY: AA Big Book Study Group, 1997), pp. 198-213, 225-228, 250-252. A.A. Historian Wally P. has dipped his finger into the problems of revisionism; but, unfortunately, has also endeavored to reconcile and harmonize in one puddle—without adequate discussion of the Bible—some of A.A.'s bizarre "higher powers;" a God of "convenience;"

the Biblical views of Clarence Snyder; the revived Oxford Group assertions of 99 year old Jim Houck; Sister Ignatia's program at St. Thomas; Wilson's New Age "fourth dimension of existence," "psychic change," and "Spirit of the Universe" ideas; and some varied, but individual interpretations of the Steps in later years. The end result has not produced either a coherent or an accurate history, but rather a self-fashioned "back to basics" program of Wally's own-making—a Wally P. program which moves us all farther and farther away from the original A.A. program and closer and closer to his illusory program where, as he writes, "You take all Twelve Steps in one month. Your life changes—you never drink again." See Wally P., *Back to Basics: The Alcoholics Anonymous Beginners' Meetings*. (AZ: Faith with Works Publishing Company, 1998), p. 27.

Oxford Group member Jim Houck (a recent colleague of Wally's) is now 99 years old, got sober cold turkey just prior to Bill Wilson's date of sobriety, and is and has been, a Christian and Bible student for years and years. Jim told me this and included the remark in his endorsement of my titles: "Take God out of A.A. and you have nothing." And that seems to be the problem in much of A.A. today. I would add: "Take James, the Sermon, and 1 Corinthians out of our history, and then you can accurately tell me that all you have left is largely psychic changes, fourth dimensions, higher powers, self-made religion, absurd names for God, and half-baked prayers—the very nonsense that Rev. Sam Shoemaker courageously decried in talks to AAs themselves" at their 1955 and 1960 International Conventions.

I can verify from extensive personal attendance and activity within A.A. for some nineteen plus years that Bob P. and the Canadian trustee are correct in their observations. In my fifteen plus years of travel and investigation, as well as participation in many types of meetings and conferences, I have seen the following: (1) Alcoholics screened and thrown out of closed meetings. (2) The prohibition at A.A. meetings of non-Conference approved books, flyers, and even the Bible. (3) Striking from the rolls A.A. groups which study the Bible, study Emmet Fox, place the Bible in an A.A. meeting, or invite speakers who tell of our Biblical roots. (4) Banning from historical websites and chat-groups the remarks of those who tell of our Christian beginnings. (5) Letters written on A.A. stationary which attempt to intimidate AAs and groups in regard to symbols, publications, book placement at meetings, and religious expressions. (6) Litigation and litigious communications emanating from GSO, attempting to penalize the recalcitrant and to impose uniformity. This just has to be due, in part, to inaccurate historical writings and information; unwanted professionalism injected into our Fellowship; irreligious prejudice; or just plain egotistical aspirations for control—no matter what the end product. As A.A. buys this stuff, its success rates deteriorate, splinter groups proliferate, and older members just plain leave! That's not to mention the tens of thousands who are denied access to the flavor, the history, the open-mindedness, the altruism, and the autonomous service in early A.A. itself.

I often recall from my research of early A.A. the expression "No pay for soul surgery." It stemmed from the Oxford Group and became embodied in A.A.'s

Twelfth Step work (particularly that involving Dr. Bob and over 5,000 people he helped without charge). Plainly, it meant, "We don't get paid for our service." By contrast, we AAs today pay for the seemingly endless production line of "Conference Approved" and GSO published books and literature (which are then frequently edited, revised, and reprinted); we pay for offices; we pay for administration; we pay for conventions; and we pay for litigation. All this comes from annual revenues, largely derived from book sales that were in the neighborhood of ten million dollars a year not long ago. Such overhead at the paid level of service propels the hierarchy to fear its own end; others to insure more control; and still others toward promoting their own private interpretations. And it has driven the facts out of most of our histories facts about God, facts about Christianity, facts about the Bible, facts about our founders, facts about what they read and did, facts about the sources of our ideas, and facts about cure!

The all-too-numerous revisionist historical writings and doctrines today: I have made a search many times. I have many, varied, historical and research books flowing my way with great regularity. I have looked at the historical writings of most of the best-known A.A. writers, those who don't work for A.A. General Services. These are fine people, good writers, and researchers. But our real spiritual history is missing from their work. I'm not one of those frustrated, disgruntled believers in A.A. and there are many who think there is some kind of conspiracy to eliminate God, the Bible, Jesus Christ, and the Holy Spirit from A.A. Actually, there are writers like Ernest Kurtz who think there is some kind of movement to shove God, the

Bible, Jesus Christ, and the Holy Spirit back "into" A.A. Instead, I am one of those who simply can't understand how or why so many good writers just don't write or talk about or analyze the real Bible roots of A.A.

Let's be specific. The following widely disseminated works appear to contain absolutely no, or certainly very little significant mention of, A.A. in company with the Bible, or of the Book of James as far as our actual and original recovery program is concerned: See Mel B., *My Search For Bill W.*, (MN: Hazelden, 2000); Mel B., *New Wine: The Spiritual Roots of the Twelve Step Miracle*. (MN: Hazelden, 1991); *Bill W.: My First 40 Years*. (MN: Hazelden, 2000); Sally Brown and David R. Brown. *A Biography of Mrs. Marty Mann: The First Lady of Alcoholics Anonymous*. (MN: Hazelden, 2001); Robert Fitzgerald, S. J., *The Soul of Sponsorship: The Friendship of Fr. Ed Dowling, S.J. and Bill Wilson in Letters*. (MN: Hazelden, 1995); Francis Hartigan, *Bill W.: A Biography of Alcoholics Anonymous Cofounder Bill Wilson*. (NY: St. Martin's Press, 2000); Ernest Kurtz, *Not-God: A History of Alcoholics Anonymous*, Exp ed. (MN: Hazelden, 1991); Matthew J. Raphael, *Bill W. and Mr. Wilson: The Legend and Life of A.A.'s Co-founder*. (Amherst: University of Massachusetts Press, 2000); Robert Thomsen, *Bill W.* (NY: Perennial Library, Harper & Row, 1975); Tom White, *Bill W.: A Different Kind of Hero: The Story of Alcoholics Anonymous*. (PA: Boyds Mill Press, 2003); William L. White, *Slaying The Dragon: The History of Addiction Treatment and Recovery in America* (IL: Chestnut Health Systems/Lighthouse Institute, 1998); and the about-to-be released Lois *Wilson Story*. I confess I haven't read the recent Susan Cheever title, but I've heard nothing that suggests this later writer covers our full story accurately or adequately.

I should point out that I mention the lacuna in the foregoing historical writings not because they do or do not cover their selected subject matter accurately, but because their omissions have generated the common impression that today's A.A. is not religious, not Christian, and no longer oriented to its long-proclaimed statement that "God could and would if He were sought." Instead, they have portrayed a revisionist, universalized, sanitized, wimpy A.A. with an emphasis on not-drinking and going to meetings, but at meetings where you can believe in anything, "Something," or nothing at all. And what a case these writers, many of them professionals, have made for treatment, prevention, therapy, and rehabilitation centers. Also for para-church groups where people don't believe in something or nothing at all, but rather in the Bible, Jesus Christ, and healing. Also, ironically, for atheist or humanist groups which still think that A.A. is a religion, is too religious, and is ineffective, compared to therapeutic techniques.

If we buy all this, why would we even want to look at the Book of James in an A.A. history work! In a very real sense, the revisionist approaches leave faith—the faith of Jesus Christ that early AAs had—behind. They pass the victory wreath on to those who merely talk today about "works"—whether the "works" are treatment, therapy, para-churches that depend on 12 Steps, or secular "self-help" programs.

The Emergence of Non-AA "Twelve Step Bibles":
Shortly after I began my research into the Biblical roots of A.A., I ran into a very sad trend that suddenly had been magnified into huge proportions. In the zeal of the early 1990's for treatment programs, rehabs, therapy,

and recovery books, several major religious publishers decided to formulate a new type of A.A. presumably for Christians—but an A.A. that depended as much on Twelve Steps as it did on God and His Word. Regrettably, their ponderous works simply shoved the Bible into the Twelve Steps instead of recording and commenting on the Biblical history of A.A. itself and the Bible's contributions to the Steps. As with the revisionist historians, however, there seemed to be a large and undue focus on the "Oxford Group roots" of A.A. to the exclusion of the Bible itself. The publishers rammed into their "recovery" Bibles page after page of Step commentaries attached to supposedly relevant verses. The writers seem to be more recognized for their Ph.D.'s in psychology than for their D. Min's in religion. Seeming to respond enthusiastically to these tomes, para-church groups, often calling themselves "Christ-centered" Twelve Step Fellowships, began wide use of these "Twelve Step Bibles." The publishers sold a chunk of the religious community on the idea that the Bible, without the Twelve Steps, was an ineffective recovery tool. The three "Twelve Step" Bibles—still splattered throughout the internet book ads—that I have found most in use were: (1) *Recovery Devotional Bible* (MI: Zondervan Publishing House, 1993); (2) *Serenity: A Companion for Twelve Step Recovery* (Nashville: Thomas Nelson Publishers, 1990); (3) *The Life Recovery Bible: The Living Bible*. (IL: Tyndale House Publishers, Inc.,1992). All this work on the Bible and the apparent self-conceived effort to fit God's plan and will into the 12 Steps makes me wonder how many lives could have been saved in the last decade if these same publishing efforts had been invested into reporting on, setting forth, and teaching about the original Bible ideas—ideas that are very plain and relevant in, for example, the

Book of James. And highlighting the facts and "how" of the pioneer reliance on the Creator that epitomized early A.A.'s Christian Fellowship and astonishing cures.

It's important to acknowledge here that the "Twelve Step Bibles"—now so widely owned and circulated—*can* be a useful part of your history study. Take *The Life Recovery Bible*, for example. Look at its material on James at page 1401 to 1410. There are comments on just about every verse and some general observations about James. They are, of course, indicative of the religious views of the editors and not necessarily the views that early AAs took. Moreover, if you hold to the proposition that no Scripture is or should be of any "private interpretation," and that it is given us by "inspiration of God," and is to be "rightly divided," then your work with these Bibles has scarce begun. See 2 Peter 20-21; 2 Timothy 3:16-17; 2 Timothy 2:15. I personally believe you'll get far more out of prayer and direct study of the Bible than you will out of commentaries about it, however sincere their intent and diligent their analysis may be. On the other hand, don't throw out the baby with the bathwater. Any version of the Bible can help understanding. And the editors of these Bibles seem to be scholars and writers also familiar with the recovery scene. In fact, I personally know the two Executive Editors of *The Life Recovery Bible*. Both have worked in the recovery field for a long time. One is an ordained minister, and both have doctorates.

In a sense, I have just highlighted the omission James, the substitutions added in its place, and the results of leaving it behind. Now for James itself.

Identifiable Spillovers in A.A.'s Big Book and 12 Steps from the Book of James

To avoid repeating materials in the next two sections, I'll state first that there are many quotes, references, and ideas in the Book of James that regularly appeared in early A.A. writing and practices. The following are a few:

"Faith without works is dead" was practically the father verse among the ideas that bounced around early A.A. from James. The verse itself is quoted or paraphrased several times in the Big Book. The verse was allegedly the favorite Bible verse of Anne Smith, Dr. Bob's wife (though that theory has not been documented).The verse was allegedly Bill Wilson's favorite, along with the Book of James. And expressions said to have come from this verse were and are common in A.A. Thus Wilson named his Big Book promotional and publishing corporation "Works Publishing Company." The shortest sentence in A.A.'s Big Book is "It works." Big Book Chapter Five is titled "How it Works;" and the first part of that chapter is read at the beginning of many A.A. meetings. Most every A.A. meeting ends with the formation of a circle in which the members join hands, join in reciting either the Lord's Prayer or the Serenity Prayer, and conclude by shaking their arms up and down and shouting, "Keep coming back. It Works." See also Kurtz, *Not-God*, *supra*, pp. 68-69; Raphael, *Bill W. and Mr. Wilson*, *supra*, pp. 116-17.

"Confess your faults one to another" though modified and amplified by the Oxford Group, by Rev. Sam Shoemaker, and by Bill's Fifth Step and its discussion language—James 5:16 has been almost universally acknowledged to be the basic source idea from James 5:16 for Step Five.

"But the tongue can no man tame: it is an unruly evil full of deadly poison"—In his last talk to AAs, Dr. Bob cautioned the fellowship to "guard that erring member the tongue." And Anne Smith made similar comments in the spiritual journal she kept and shared with early AAs and their families.

"Thou shalt love thy neighbor as thyself"—Of course, this sentence can be found in many Bible passages in addition to the one in James. It is called "The royal law according to the scripture" in James 2:8. And the verse is paraphrased in the Big Book.

"Father of lights"—a reference to Almighty God in James 1:17. Bill quoted this phrase, but misspelled it in his Big Book. He often mentioned it in talks to A.A. members. He spoke of the "Father of lights" who presides over us all.

The words and phrases in the following sections will illustrate how many other basic A.A. ideas came from the Book of James, though they were not actually quotes of chapter and verse and did not provide appropriate attribution.

Specific Pioneer A.A. Ideas from James

Again, to avoid undue repetition of the detailed study in the following James section, we will merely highlight here some of the key James ideas that seem to resemble words and phrases AAs adopted.

Patience.

Avoiding temptation.

Asking wisdom of God with unwavering faith.

Enduring temptation.

Recognizing that resisting temptation is man's responsibility, not God's.

Laying aside wrath and filthiness and receiving the Word of God with meekness.

Being a "doer of the word," not a hearer only.

Purporting to be religious, yet failing to bridle the tongue.

Confirming that "pure" and "undefiled religion" includes visiting the fatherless and widows and keeping yourself unspotted from the world.

Not being a respecter of persons in well-doing.

Fulfilling the royal law to love thy neighbor as thyself.

Keeping all God's commandments, not just the ones you like.

Accompanying faith with works.

Taming the tongue.

Recognizing that envying and strife are the product of "devilish" "wisdom."

Realizing that wisdom from above is pure, peaceable, gentle, full of mercy and good fruits, and without partiality or hypocrisy.

Realizing that asking amiss in prayer comes from asking to consume the object of your prayer upon your own lusts.

Knowing God resists the proud, but gives grace to the humble.

Submitting yourselves to God. Resisting the devil, and believing he will flee from you.

Drawing near to God knowing He will draw near to you.

Humbling yourselves in the sight of the Lord, and knowing He shall lift you up.

Avoiding speaking evil of, or judging, other brethren.

Saying that if the Lord will, you will live, and do this or that.

Knowing you are to do works that God's defines as good, and that doing what is not good—as that is defined in the Bible—is sin.

Holding no grudges.

Eschewing swearing.

If you are sick, summoning the elders of the church and letting them pray over you.

Believing this prayer of faith shall save the sick, and the Lord shall raise you up and forgive your sins.

Confessing your faults one to another

Praying for one another that you may be healed.

Believing that the effectual fervent prayer of a righteous man avails much.

Knowing that he who converts a sinner from the error of his way shall save a soul from death, and shall hide a multitude of sins.

You can find these principles in the writings of Rev. Sam Shoemaker, in various issues of *The Upper Room*, in the pages of *The Runner's Bible*, in Oxford Group writings, and in much of the Christian literature early AAs read with regularity. Many of these writings cite the correlative verses in James. And those of you who are steeped in A.A. sayings and thought should readily recognize the parallels.

A Review of the Bible's Book of James as It Reached A.A.

Both Bill W. and Dr. Bob stated many times that Jesus' Sermon on the Mount contained the underlying philosophy of A.A. Furthermore, our research has demonstrated how many words, phrases, and ideas in A.A. were borrowed from that Sermon. However, of probably much greater importance (than the Sermon) in the day-by-day thinking of early A.A., was the Book of James. It was much studied by A.A.'s co-founders. Quotes and ideas from the Apostle James can be found throughout the Big Book and in A.A. literature. As shown, the Book of James was considered so important that many favored calling the A.A. fellowship the "James Club" *(DR. BOB and the Good Oldtimers,* p. 71; *Pass It On,* p. 147). And even the most fundamental phrases in A.A., such as "It Works" and Bill Wilson's own "Works Publishing Company" (which published the First Edition of the Big Book), probably have their origin in the "Faith without works is dead" phrases in the Book of James (See: Nell Wing, *Grateful to Have Been There,* pp. 70-71).

Let's therefore undertake a review the Book of James, chapter by chapter, and verse by verse. As we do so, we will point to traces of that book which we believe can be found in, or probably influenced the text of, the Big Book. At the outset, we would report that as our research into the Biblical roots of A.A. has progressed, so has our understanding of some root sources that previously went unnoticed.

A.A.'s lack of commentaries on James that were similar to, and available to assist study of, those available and used on Corinthians and the Sermon on the mount: Not only did pioneer AAs have the Bible itself to study, when it came to the Sermon on the Mount and First Corinthians, but they had and used excellent commentaries by Henry Drummond, Samuel M. Shoemaker, Oswald Chambers, Glenn Clark, E. Stanley Jones, and Emmet Fox—all of which contained popular comments on the two Bible parts.

We could find no similar commentary that the pioneers used with the Book of James, despite A.A.'s specific emphasis on James. Finally, in our search for James reference materials, we studied again and again the spiritual literature early AAs read.

Relevance of The Runner's Bible: We noticed in *The Runner's Bible* the frequency with which all the books and chapters that Dr. Bob called "absolutely essential" (Matthew chapters 5-7, 1 Corinthians 13, and James) were there mentioned. We particularly noticed the frequency with which *The Runner's Bible* mentioned and discussed verses from the Book of James. Hence our reader will find many references to *The Runner's Bible* in the footnotes of our title *The Good Book and The Big Book;* for we believe that the little "Runner's" devotional book may have provided Dr. Bob, Anne Smith, and perhaps even Bill Wilson, with much of the fodder that caused them to focus on James and to conclude, if they did, that James was their "favorite" book of the Bible. In a phone conversation with the author in 1995, from his home in Texas, Dr. Bob's son stated that *The Runner's Bible* (a little Biblical devotional book) was often used by those pioneers who wanted a quick and easy source for Biblical ideas in which they were interested. Perhaps, then, that book became a reference source for Dr. Bob, Anne, and even Bill Wilson when they were studying the pertinent Biblical ideas they extracted from 1 Corinthians 13, the Sermon on the Mount, and particularly James.

Relevance of United Christian Endeavor Practices

Take some time to study the Christian Endeavor material in our appendix. Realize too that we are far from through with our investigation and research of the principles and practices of United Christian Endeavor, in which Dr. Bob was a participant in his youth. But we know enough now to be sure that Akron's "Christian Fellowship" far more resembled United Christian Endeavor than it did the Oxford Group. And we know a great deal about the Endeavor's Confession of Christ, conversion meetings, Bible studies, prayer meetings, Quiet Hour, and emphasis on love and service. These principles and practices closely parallel those of the original A.A. pioneer group. They don't resemble those commonly found in the Oxford Group.

Of even more significance here is the fact that each Christian Endeavor group kept a log of its programs. We know for sure their emphasis on the Sermon on the Mount and on 1 Corinthians 13; and we recently found a log detailing a study of the Book of James. For now, therefore, the question is how many other groups did likewise. Also whether Dr. Bob's own St. Johnsbury Christian Endeavor group engaged in such a study or studies during the several years of Bob's membership and participation.

Now let's look at the chapters in James—one by one.

James Chapter 1

1. **Patience.** Chapter One is not the only chapter in the Book of James which mentions patience. Nor is it the only portion of the Bible that stresses patience. But we've noted that James was a favored Biblical source in early A.A., and James 1:3-4 do state:

> Knowing *this,* that the trying of your faith worketh patience. But let patience have *her* perfect work, that ye may be perfect and entire, wanting nothing.

Patience certainly wound up as one of the most frequently mentioned spiritual principles in the Big Book (Fourth Ed., pp. 67, 70, 83, 111, 118, 163). And patience figured heavily as a *sine qua non* for application of the three absolutely essential beginning points for the Akron newcomer: Patience in overcoming the throes of acute withdrawal. Patience in dealing with the roller-coaster days of delayed withdrawal. And, of course, patience in recognizing that there is no progress toward a cure that does not necessitate patience in resisting temptation and remaining abstinent.

2. **Asking wisdom of God with unwavering believing**. James 1:5-8 state:

> If any of you lack wisdom, let him ask of God, that giveth to all *men* liberally, and upbraideth not; and it shall be given him.
>
> But let him ask in faith, nothing wavering. For he that wavereth is like a wave of the sea driven with the wind and tossed.
>
> For let not that man think that he shall receive anything of the Lord. A double minded man *is* unstable in all his ways.

Asking for God's direction and strength and receiving "Guidance" from Him, are major themes in both the Old and New Testaments. They were important Oxford Group ideas as well. We therefore discussed them at length in our titles on the Oxford Group and on Anne Smith's spiritual journal. Certainly the Big Book, including the Eleventh Step itself, is filled with such Guidance concepts (Fourth Ed., pp.13, 46, 49, 62-63, 69-70, 76, 79-80, 83, 84-88, 100, 117, 120, 124, 158, 164). Seeking God's guidance, wisdom, and strength—without giving in to doubt or faltering—is vital in resisting temptation and finding a safe and Godly way out and through the shoals.

3. Resisting temptation. It should surprise no one that AAs of yesteryear and of today are interested in resisting temptation, and having the power to do that that power being the power of God. James 1:12-16 state:

> Blessed *is* the man that endureth temptation: for when he is tried, he shall receive the crown of life, which the Lord hath promised to those that love him.

> Let no man say when he is tempted, I am tempted of God: for God cannot be tempted with evil, neither tempteth he any man:
>
> But every man is tempted when he is drawn away of his own lust and enticed.
>
> Then when lust hath conceived, it bringeth forth sin: and sin, when it is finished, bringeth forth death.
>
> Do not err, my beloved brethren.

Patient, relentless, resistance to temptation accompanied by action in obedience to God's wisdom and guidance were keys to cure.

3a. A special note on resisting temptation (with God's help), being cured, and remaining cured.

My personal view is that the foregoing verses in James 1:12-16, offer much insight into the *cure* of alcoholism and other life-controlling afflictions as early AAs saw the solution when they so often claimed they were "cured." See Dick B., *Cured: Proven Help for Alcoholics and Addicts*, and Richard K. *So You Think that Drunks Cannot Be Cured*.

Man's job is to resist the devilBBsays James in one verse. Man is to endure temptation when he is tried, says another. When he is tempted, he cannot blame the temptation on GodBBwho cannot be tempted and does not tempt. Man can be tempted by being drawn away of his own lust and enticed. James 3:15-16 speaks of a "wisdom [that] descendeth not from above, but is earthly, sensual, and devilish." And, says James, when the enticement produces lustful [and excessive] thoughts and behavior [such as getting drunk and drunkenness], it can and should be recognized as sin, and sin as the producer of death.

For the "real" alcoholic (who is willing to go to any lengths to beat alcohol), the "devilish," tempting thoughts must be resisted and expelled. The early A.A. prescription required much more than mere abstinence from drinking and going to 12 Step meetings. In fact there were no steps and were no meetings. That's not in the Book of James. The enjoined failure to resist occurred when a man failed to submit to God, resist the devil, humble himself in the sight of God, and appropriately believe to be lifted up and out by his Creator.

Thus 2 Corinthians 10:5 calls for casting down human reasoning and "every high thing that exalteth itself against the knowledge of God, and bringing into captivity every thought to the obedience of Christ."

We are the ones who are to control the thoughts. 1 Corinthians 10:13 points out:

> There hath no temptation taken you but such as is common to man; but God is faithful, who will not suffer you to be tempted above that ye are able; but will with the temptation also make a way to escape, that ye may be able to bear it.

To be "cured" of what Dr. Bob called the curse of alcoholism, I believe, we need to recognize that the temptation to disobey God is common and, as Paul wrote, "Now, if I do that I would not, it is no more I that do it, but sin that dwelleth in me. I find then a law, that, when I would do good, evil is present with me" (Romans 7:20-21).

The serpent tempted Eve to disobey God, and she did—reaping spiritual death for herself and Adam, who joined her in disobedience (Genesis 2:16-3:24; Romans 5:12-21). The devil tempted Jesus for forty days; but Jesus resisted each offer and challenge from the devil by standing on God's Word and quoting it to the devil (Luke 4:1-13)—who, by the way, earned a title as "the tempter" (1 Thessalonians 3:5). And the Lord's Prayer asks that God lead no disciples to be tempted, but rather that He deliver them from evil (Matthew 6:13).

In many verses of the Bible, God makes it clear that His will is against drunkenness (*e.g.*: Galatians 5:21). In Ephesians 5:18, He commands: "And be not drunk with wine, wherein is excess." Drunkenness from "excessive" drinking is, according to God's admonition, to be abhorred. Compare the comments in Jerry G. Dunn, *God is for the Alcoholic* (Chicago: Moody Press, 1965, pp. 70-72) with those in Philip Tate. Alcohol: *How To Give It Up and Be Glad You Did* (AZ: See Sharp Press, 1997).

Jerry Dunn makes the case that the Bible doesn't tell anyone *not* to drink but that it does establish that *drunkenness* is sin. According to Dunn, there is also a strong case that a Christian should abstain; but that is a matter of choice. Tate, on the other hand, contends that you can give up drinking by using rational thinking—without resorting to A.A. or religion. Again, a case is made for *choice* and how to implement it. But recognize that despite the fact that these two writers come from completely different starting points, both make the case for choice and how to implement it.

Dr. Bob took several stern, simple positions about the alcoholic, abstinence, temptation, and drinking. These views had nothing to do with cure or no cure. They had to do with what the real alcoholic inevitably does after the first drink. *DR. BOB, supra*, tells us:

> Doc would hit first with the medical facts.... He also emphasized that it was a *fatal* illness and that the only way a man could recover from it— or rather not die from it—was not to take a drink to start with. That was the basis of the whole thing. In turn, we were pounding it into each other. After this, we got to the spiritual part (p. 113)

> He'd say, [Dr. Bob would say:] Stay away from that place [Stone's grill with a back bar]. They have got nothing in there that you can't get somewhere else, whether it's food, cigarettes, or a Coke. Remembering his own disastrous trip to Atlantic City and Bill's experiment with keeping liquor on the sideboard to prove it was no longer a temptation, Dr. Bob advocated that members stay in dry places whenever possible. "You don't ask the Lord not to lead you into temptation, then turn around and walk right into it," he said (p. 281)

> He [Dr. Bob] told me that before I could be honest with him or my sponsor or anyone else, I had to "get honest with that joker in the glass. . . . When you shave tomorrow, get honest with the man who looks back at you from the looking glass." Dr. Bob said that even then, it wasn't "Easy Does It" for him. "In the morning, when I get up and put my feet on the cold floor. . . I have a battle all day to stay away from that drink. You know, Dan, there were times in the

early days of Alcoholics Anonymous when I passed those saloons that I had to pull my car over to the side of the curb and say a prayer" (p. 282)

Another thing Dr. Bob put quite simply: "The first one will get you." According to John R., he kept repeating that (p. 227).

Dr. Bob was stressing willpower, abstinence, and resisting temptation—not the "powerless" position incorporated in later A.A. thinking and writing.

Was Dr. Bob cured?

You decide: He never took a drink after June 10, 1935 (the agreed date of his sobriety). He had a strong relationship with God, and practiced strong fellowship with God. Having been burned once in Atlantic City at the beginning, he consistently stayed away from temptation and that first drink. He spent the happiest years of his life, with wife and family, after he quit drinking for good. Sounds to me like he was cured and enjoying an abundant spiritual life.

The original Akron program insisted emphatically that "An alcoholic must realize that he is an alcoholic, incurable from a medical viewpoint, and that he must never again drink anything with alcohol in it. . . . [he must] want to stop drinking permanently" (DR. BOB, supra, p. 131). That means, concerning temptation, that any lingering thoughts about letting temptation make a nest in our mind and motivate our behavior must be, and can be, cast out if our behavior is to conform with God's will (2 Corinthians 10:5). Tempting thoughts need to be resisted. They need to be expelled.

And we need to believe what God says in the Book of James—we are to submit ourselves to God; resist the devil; and be assured by God own Word and declaration that the devil *will* flee. And he does! We need to believe that God will lift us up and out. We need to believe that we can escape the net and bear the temptation with the help of our faithful Creator.

3b. Willpower: Resisting temptation certainly requires willpower, believing, praying, changing behavior, changing ideas, changing habits, changing hobbies, changing cronies, and changing hangouts. See some of the suggestions about sound thinking and actions that are made by the "rational recovery" folks (Tate, *How to Give it Up, supra*). Facing up to, and resisting, temptation is not a matter of bravado. People who are allergic to strawberries shouldn't eat strawberries. They don't need to be brave, just abstinent. People who get a bad, stinging rash from touching nettles shouldn't touch nettles. They don't need to be brave—just willful about avoidance. People who break out in blisters when they brush against poison oak should stay away from poison oak. Again, no bravery involved—just sane thinking and sane actions. It's not a question of "cure" or "no cure;" "recovered" or "not recovered;" a "daily reprieve or no daily reprieve." Fear or no fear, abstinence involves the will to be and become sufficiently sane in thinking that you don't walk into the lair of a hungry, ferocious, roaring lion. Expecting peace, quiet, safety, and joy. One seemingly curious A.A. motto is "Think. Think. Think." And years back, I wondered what it meant. I asked around the fellowship and got no answer. I'm not sure anyone knows, but Joe McQ., of Big Book Seminar repute, suggested to me during a visit with him in Little Rock that it means: "Use your head."

You are the one who has to decide, "I quit." You are the one who has to be determined to "do anything to stay sober." You are the one who has to reject the tempting thoughts—to abstain, to reach out for help, to resist, and to ask for God's help. As Bill Wilson often said, A.A. has no monopoly on God. Nor does it offer the only way to get sober. Nor does it reject the idea that you may think you can later "drink like a gentleman." It simply suggests a way out of that thinking.

You can be cured of the curse of alcoholism, but you are nuts for sure if you start drinking and think that the tempter, the temptation, and the return of all the old stuff will not get you. Sanely thinking about what excessive drinking did to you can be an instrument of success. Failure to think that way can be an assurance of failure. God's help, the "use of your head," the application of willpower, a strong belief in God's power, a real request to God for His help, and the resolute changing of your old behavior, can and do produce success. These elements have for me. They did for the Pioneers. And the Pioneers tried to tell us that these suggested ideas could assure a cure for you.

4. Every good and perfect gift comes from God, the Father of lights.
James 1:17 states:

> Every good gift and every perfect gift is from above, and cometh down from The Father of lights, with whom is no variableness, neither shadow of turning.

Bill seemed to be referring to this verse when he wrote on page 14 of *Alcoholics Anonymous*, 4th ed.:

> I must turn in all things to the Father of Light [sic] who presides over us all [Alcoholics Anonymous, 1st ed., correctly says "the Father of Lights," p. 23.]

Bill made the same reference to our Creator, the Father of lights, who presides over us all, in Appendix I of *Alcoholics Anonymous*, 4th ed.:

> This to the end that our great blessings may never spoil us; that we shall forever live in thankful contemplation of Him who presides over us all (p. 566).

The "Him" who presides over us all was, of course, James 1:17's "Father of lights"--the Creator, Yahweh, our one true living God.

There are devilish, tempting thoughts available for your choice any time. There are also unchanging good and perfect thoughts from Yahweh our God. We are the ones to choose which we will allow to guide our actions.

5. Let every man be slow to speak, slow to wrath. James 1:19-20 state:

> Wherefore, my beloved brethren, let every man be swift to hear, slow to   speak, slow to wrath: For the wrath of man worketh not the righteousness of God.

This same verse is quoted in *The Runner's Bible* and seems quite relevant to the Big Book's injunction, "If we were to live, we had to be free of anger. . . . God save me from being angry" (Fourth Edition, pp. 66-67).

The angry person frequently lets his guard down. He yields to temptation and often rejects reasonable thinking. The angry person is beginning with a focus on devilish thoughts, instead of those which, as James puts it, come down from above.

6. Be ye doers of the word, and not hearers only.
James 1:21-22 state:

> Wherefore lay apart all filthiness and superfluity of naughtiness, and receive with meekness the engrafted word, which is able to save your souls.

> But be ye doers of the word, and not hearers only, deceiving your own selves.

Reverend Sam Shoemaker, whom Bill W. called an A.A. co-founder, made this comment on the foregoing:

> I think St. James's meaning is made much clearer in Dr. Moffatt's translation, "Act on the Word, instead of merely listening to it." Try it out in experiment, and prove it by its results otherwise you only fool yourself into believing that you have the heart of religion when you haven't (Shoemaker, *The Gospel According to You,* pp. 44-55).

In the same chapter, Shoemaker also pointed out that prayer is often more a struggle to find God than the enjoyment of Him and cooperation with His will. He added that "God is and is a Rewarder of them that seek Him." (See Shoemaker, *The Gospel According to You,* p. 47; and Hebrews 11:6).

I have not found specific or similar language to that of James 1:21-22 in the Big Book; but A.A. declares over and over that A.A. is a program of *action,* that probably no human power can relieve a person of his alcoholism, and "That God could and would if He were *sought"* (4the ed., p. 60, emphasis added). A.A.'s program emphasizes action in the experiment of faith it adopted from John 7:17*seeking* God by *following* the path that leads to a relationship with God. James 1:22 enjoins *doing* God's will as expressed in His Word not merely listening to it. James was an Akron favorite. Shoemaker was a Wilson favorite. "Faith without works" was a Big Book favorite; and it therefore seems quite reasonable to believe, and altogether possible, that A.A.'s emphasis on *action* might well have derived largely from James 1:21-22.

A "hearer" may very well receive and even consider acting on a siren call. A "doer" has heard the Word, has learned the difference between devilish calls and calls from God; and, as a doer of the Word, he acts on the latter.

7. Pure religion and undefiled before God . . . to visit the fatherless and widows in their affliction. James 1:27 states:

> Pure religion and undefiled before God and the Father is this, To visit the fatherless and widows in their affliction, *and* to keep oneself unspotted from the world.

At the very least, this verse bespeaks unselfishness and helpfulness to others which were cardinal A.A. principles particularly the principles embodied in Step Twelve. In fact, that's the point made in one of early A.A.'s pamphlets:

> And all we need to do in the St. James passage is to substitute the word "Alcoholic" for "Fatherless and Widows" and we have Step Twelve (*Spiritual Milestones*, AA of Akron, pp. 12-13).

AAs pledge themselves to obey and do God's will. They are also taught to strengthen their obedience with Godly deeds that will also remind them of the deadly results that come from yielding to temptation. Their unique method is through helping other afflicted drunks and trying to keep their own houses clean.

James Chapter 2

Chapter Two of the Book of James may have made two direct and major contributions to the language of the Big Book and also to A.A.'s philosophy. Those two contributions were "Love thy neighbor as thyself" and "Faith without works is dead."

1. Love thy neighbor as thyself. James 2:8 states:

> If ye fulfill the royal law according to the scripture, Thou shalt love thy neighbor as thyself, ye do well.

This commandment to "Love thy neighbor" exists in other parts of both the Old and New Testaments. Thus, when the Big Book incorporated this phrase, there is no assurance that the quote is from James rather than from another Bible verse to the same effect (*e.g.*, Rom. 13:9; Gal. 5:14). But the Big Book certainly does state:

> Then you will know what it means to give of yourself that others may survive and rediscover life. You will learn the full meaning of "Love thy neighbor as thyself" (Fourth ed., p. 153).

Such Big Book remarks point out to the recovered alcoholic that the spiritual objective of loving his neighbor can certainly be realized by the helping act.

The Book of James is very probably the specific source of this Biblical quote since Dr. Bob, early AAs, and Bill Wilson himself spoke with such frequency about "love" and tolerance as the code of A.A. *and* the Book of James as AAs' favorite book.

2. Faith without works is dead. Said to be the favorite verse of Anne Smith and perhaps the origin of many expressions in A.A. concerning "works," this sentence, or variations of it, appears several times in Chapter Two of the Book of James. For example, James 2:20 states:

> But wilt thou know, 0 vain man, that faith without works is dead?

"Faith without works" as a phrase, and as an A.A. "action" concept, is quoted or referred to many times in the Big Book (4th ed., pp. 14-15, 76, 88, 93, 97). A.A.'s original Oxford Group connection also put emphasis on these James verses concerning the importance of witnessing and "sharing for witness" as they called it.

And sometimes, I believe, A.A. today has put far too much emphasis on "works" (often calling it "service) yet ignored and forgotten the "faith" part. The "faith" of pioneer A.A. is the faith of Jesus Christ. Galatians 2:16 says:

> Knowing that a man is not justified by the works of the law, but by the faith of Jesus Christ, even we have believed in Jesus Christ, that we might be justified by the faith of Christ, and not by the works of the law: for by the works of the law shall no flesh be justified.

As Galatians explains, the Bible is not talking about faith in terms of words or acts of kindness and good deeds. The empowering faith—the acquittal of guilt—comes by grace, and not by what man has observed or done. It comes because God blesses His kids with unearned rewards, not because they placed their faith in His words and prescribed works, but because they received their faith, despite their words and works, because of what their Lord Jesus Christ and his faith had done for them.

3. Helping Others. It hardly requires citation or documentation to state that A.A.'s cardinal objective is to help others. Specifically, other drunks who reach out for help. Early on, the Big Book states, "Our very lives, as ex-problem drinkers, depend upon our constant thought of others and how we may help meet their needs" (Fourth ed., p. 20). Later, it continues at page 89:

> Practical experience shows that nothing will so much insure immunity from drinking as

intensive work with other alcoholics. It works
when other activities fail. This is our *twelfth
suggestion*: Carry this message to other
alcoholics! You can help when no one else can.
You can secure their confidence when others
fail.

The basic spiritual backdrop is underlined in Chapter 2
of James. That chapter begins by talking of the love of
God which decrees Godly works, beginning with verses
1 to 7 which say:

My brethren, have not the faith of our Lord
Jesus Christ, the Lord of glory, with respect of
persons. For if there come unto your assembly a
man with a gold ring, in goodly apparel, and
there come in also a poor man in vile raiment;
And ye have respect to him that weareth the
gay clothing, and say unto him, Sit thou here in
a good place; and say to the poor, Stand thou
there, or sit here under my footstool: Are ye not
then partial in yourselves, and are become
judges of evil thoughts? Hearken, my beloved
brethren, Hath not God chosen the poor of this
world rich in faith, and heirs of the kingdom
which he hath promised to them that love him?
But ye have despised the poor. Do not rich men
oppress you, and draw you before the judgment
seats? Do not they blaspheme that worthy
name by the which ye are called?

James 2:15-16 state this principle of unconditional,
undiscriminating good deeds very well:

If a brother or sister be naked, and destitute of
daily food, And one of you say unto them,
Depart in peace, be ye warmed and filled;

> notwithstanding ye give them not those things which are needful to the body; what doth it profit? Even so, faith, if it hath not works, is dead, being alone.

And every alcoholic who has helped one of his miserable, suffering, destitute brothers in need will, I believe, instantly relate to those verses and hence to the importance the early AAs attached to James itself.

4. The Ten Commandments. Again! James 2:10-11 state:

> For whosoever shall keep the whole law, and yet offend in one *point,* he is guilty of all. For he that said, Do not commit adultery, said also, Do not kill. Now if thou commit no adultery, yet if thou kill, thou art become a transgressor of the law.

Believers are not accorded the liberty of picking and choosing which of God's commandments are acceptable and worthy of their attention. They are told to obey all. Whatever one may think is representative of, or acceptable in today's A.A., he will find language about and references to the Ten Commandments with great frequency in *early* A.A. You will see more of this same point in our review of the Sermon on the Mount.

James Chapter 3

1. Taming the tongue. In his Farewell Address to A.A., Dr. Bob said:

> Let us also remember to guard that erring member the tongue, and if we must use it, let's use it with kindness and consideration and tolerance *(DR. BOB and the Good Oldtimers,* p. 338).

A major portion of James chapter 3 is devoted to the trouble that can be caused by an untamed tongue. Following are a few verses emphasizing the point:

> Even so the tongue is a little member and boasteth great things.
>
> Behold, how great a matter a little fire kindleth! And the tongue *is* a fire, a world of iniquity; so is the tongue among our members that it defileth the whole body, and setteth on fire the course of nature; and *it is* set on fire of hell.
>
> But the tongue can no man tame; it is an unruly evil, full of deadly poison.
>
> Out of the same mouth proceedeth blessing and cursing. My brethren, these things ought not to be (James 3:5, 6, 8, 10)

These verses are not quoted in the Big Book. But Anne Smith referred to them frequently in her journal, as did other A.A. roots sources (Dick B., *Anne Smith's Journal,* pp. 28, 44, 76, 77; Holm, *The Runner's Bible,* p. 68). But, in paraphrasing those verses, Dr. Bob seemed to be speaking of the necessity for tolerance, courtesy, consideration, and kindness in our speech and actions. James makes clear that good *conversation* should be a focus conversation, we believe, that is laced with consideration, kindness, and tolerance (See James 3:13). And these latter principles *are* very much in evidence in the Big Book (4th ed., pp. 67, 69-70, 83-84, 97, 118, 125, 135).

Outspoken fiery language incites untoward action and diminishes sound reasoning. God opposes it. And man's obedience to God's injunctions reminds that God blesses those who obey.

2. Avoidance of envy, strife, and lying. James 3:14-16 proclaim that a heart filled with envy, strife, and lies has not received *that* kind of "wisdom" from God, but rather from devilish sources. The verses state:

> But if ye have bitter envying and strife in your hearts; glory not, and lie not against the truth.
>
> This wisdom descendeth not from above, but is earthly, sensual, devilish.
>
> For where envying and strife is, there is confusion and every evil work.

"Envy" is not as much decried in the Big Book as jealousy; but a more modern translation of these King James verses equates "envy" *with* "jealousy" (*The Revised English Bible, New Testament*, p, 208). And the Big Book most assuredly condemns jealously (4th ed., pp. 37, 69, 82, 100, 119, 145, 161). In fact, the Big Book states as to jealousy *and* envy:

> Keep it always in sight that we are dealing with that most terrible human emotion jealousy (p. 82).

> The greatest enemies of us alcoholics are resentment, jealousy, envy, frustration, and fear (p. 145).

Again these "enemies" in action violate God's rules. They replace Godly wisdom with devilish thinking. They open the door to many and all the devilish behaviors that descend from devilish sources.

And as to strife, the Big Book states:

> After all, our problems were of our own making. Bottles were only a symbol. Besides, we have stopped fighting anybody or anything. We have to (4th ed., p. 103)!

James 3:17-18 talk much about making peace and the fruit of righteousness being sown in peace of them that make peace.

As seen in the quote from James 3:14, lying and dishonesty are also declared to be devilish; and one should note and compare the Big Book's frequent emphasis on grasping and developing a manner of living which "demands rigorous honesty" (4th ed., p. 58). As to all the verses in James 3:14-16, however, there is little certainty that these particular verses were an exclusive or even major source for the Big Books condemnation of envy, jealousy, strife, and dishonesty because all these traits are stated to be objectionable by many other parts of the Bible. They are resolutely condemned in God's Word.

James Chapter 4:

1. Asking amiss for selfish ends. A.A.'s writings have much to say about overcoming selfishness and self-centeredness. But the following in James 4:3 particularly eschews determined selfishness in prayer:

> Ye ask, and receive not, because ye ask amiss, that ye may consume it upon your lusts.

Several Christian A.A. sources that were favorites of Dr. Bob's discuss this verse at length. And the Big Book authors may therefore have borrowed from James 4:3, in this statement:

> We ask especially for freedom from self-will, and are careful to make no request for ourselves only. We may ask for ourselves, however, if others will be helped. We are careful never to pray for our own selfish ends. Many of us have wasted a lot of time doing that and it doesn't work (Big Book, 4th ed., p. 87).

Neither does failure to ask in accordance with God's will (See 1 John 5:14-15).

2. Humility. The Book of James has no corner on the Biblical injunction to be humble. But the importance of James, and the remarks of Reverend Samuel Shoemaker (quoted under Item 3 immediately below) suggest that the following verses from James may have been a source of the Big Book's frequent mention of humility. James 4:7, 10 state:

> Submit yourselves therefore to God. Resist the devil, and he will flee from you.

> Humble yourselves in the sight of the Lord, and he shall lift you up.

God requires that His will be sought, and He promises rewards to those who seek it.

The Big Book's Fourth Edition is filled with exhortations to be humble, with stress on humbling one's self before God, and with suggestions for humbly asking His help. Examples include:

> There I humbly offered myself to God, as I understood Him, to do with me as He would (p. 13).

> He humbly offered himself to his Maker then he knew (p. 57).

> Just to the extent that we do as we think He would have us, and humbly rely on Him, does He enable us to match calamity with serenity (p. 68).

> We constantly remind ourselves we are no longer running the show, humbly saying to ourselves many times each day "Thy will be done" (pp. 87-88).

3. Trusting God and cleaning house. James 4:8 states:

> Draw nigh to God, and he will draw nigh to you. Cleanse your hands, ye sinners; and purify your hearts, ye double minded.

The Big Book says on page 98 of the Fourth Edition:

> Burn the idea into the consciousness of every
> man that he can get well regardless of anyone.
> The only condition is that he trust in God and
> clean house.

And, in language closely paralleling that in James 4:8, the
Big Book says further that one can establish conscious
companionship with God by simply, honestly, and humbly
seeking and drawing near to Him:

> He has come to all who have honestly sought Him.
> When we drew near to Him He disclosed Himself
> to us (page 57)!

In Step Seven, the Big Book relates "cleaning house" of
one's character defects to "humbly asking" God to remove
them. The foregoing verses in James, which speak of
drawing near to God, cleansing our hearts, humbling
ourselves in His sight, and then being "lifted" up by God,
appear to have been directly involved in framing the Big
Book's Seventh Step language. In fact, many years after
the Big Book was written, Sam Shoemaker thus clarified
his understanding of the Seventh Step, in a 1964 issue of
the   *AA*   *Grapevine*:

> Sins get entangled deep within us, as some
> roots of a tree, and do not easily come loose.
> We need help, grace, the lift of a kind of divine
> derrick (Shoemaker, "Those Twelve Steps as I
> Understand Them"; *Volume II, Best of the
> Grapevine*, p. 130).

All such verses, Big Book remarks, and statements by Sam
Shoemaker illustrate that the elimination of all sins—
including yielding to temptation—are involved in changing. It
is not just the effort of man that solves the problem. It is
God's help that saves the day.

4. Taking your own inventory. James 4:11-12 state:

> Speak not evil one of another, brethren. He that speaketh evil of *his* brother, and judgeth his brother, speaketh evil of the law, and judgeth the law: but if thou judge the law, thou art not a doer of the law, but a judge.
>
> There is one lawgiver, who is able to save and to destroy: who art thou that judgest another?

Later, we discuss the importance of A.A.'s Fourth Step inventory process as it derives from relevant verses in the Sermon on the Mount which were often quoted by Oxford Group people and by Anne Smith (See Matt. 7:1-5). But the Big Book places special emphasis on this inventory process, suggesting that we examine all biblical sources for the Big Book's talk of: (1) looking "for our own mistakes," (2) asking "Where were we to blame," and (3) realizing, "The inventory was ours, not the other man's." Considering the importance to AAs of the Book of James and its insights, the foregoing James verses in James 4:11-12 probably also had an impact on the A.A. idea of avoiding judgment of another and focusing on an examination of one's *own* conduct when it comes to wrongdoing.

James Chapter 5

1. Patience. We discussed A.A.'s "patience principle" as having probably derived from James, Chapter One. As we said, however, additional stress on patience can be found in James 5:7, 8, 10, 11. There is to be patience in (a) Recognizing and enduring temptation. (b) Seeking God's help when temptation arises. (c) Resisting the "tempter"—knowing that he will yield to the power of God and flee. That's the simple answer James offers the believer.

2. Grudges (covered in A.A.'s 4th Step resentment inventory process). James 5:9 reads:

> Grudge not one against another, brethren, lest ye be condemned; behold, the judge standeth before the door.

A major portion of the Big Book's Fourth Step discussion is devoted to resentment, about which page 64 says:

> Resentment is the "number one" offender. It destroys more alcoholics than anything else. From it stem all forms of spiritual disease.

In the context of victorious living, this variety of sin is just another example of where the believer is to give place to Godly thoughts and actions instead of yielding to devilish ones.

The Big Book suggests putting resentments *on paper*making a "*grudge list*" (pp. 64-65). Oxford Group spokesman Ebenezer Macmillan wrote at length in his title *Seeking and Finding* about eliminating resentments, hatred, or the "*grudge*" that "blocks God out effectively." Rev. Sam Shoemaker also specified "grudges" as one of the "sins" to be examined in an inventory of self (Shoemaker, *Twice-Born Ministers*, p. 182). The Big Book suggests listing resentments or "grudges" as one of the four major "character defects" which block us from God; and it seems quite possible that the "grudge" language in the Big Book was influenced by James, and perhaps specifically by James 5:9.

3. Asking God's forgiveness for sins. Here and elsewhere in the Bible, we find an answer to the hopelessness and despair which so often beset the alcoholic. The Word of God offers relief to the repentant sinner—not just endless condemnation. We repeat James 5:15, which was partially quoted above. The entire verse says:

> And the prayer of faith shall save the sick, and the Lord shall raise him up; and if he have committed sins, they shall be forgiven him.

Compare the following Big Book statements about asking God's forgiveness when we fall short:

> If we are sorry for what we have done, and have the honest desire to let God take us to better things, we believe we will be forgiven and will have learned our lesson (4th ed, p. 70).

> When we retire at night, we constructively review our day.... After making our review, we ask God's forgiveness and inquire what corrective measures should be taken (4th ed., p. 86).

The foregoing Big Book quotes seem to demonstrate Bill Wilson's view that, even after their initial surrender, wrongdoers may continue sinning and therefore may still, in A.A.' s view (and with certainly the Bible's assurance), seek and receive God's forgiveness for shortcomings indulged after the initial surrender. Here again, James has no corner on the statement that God makes it possible, through forgiveness, for a believer to regain fellowship with Him. The following in 1 John 1:9 may also have been a source of such Big Book ideas:

> If we confess our sins, he is faithful and just to forgive us *our* sins, and to cleanse us from all unrighteousness.

We will further discuss forgiveness in connection with the Sermon on the Mount. It is fair to say, however, that the Book of James, 1 John, or Matthew could each, or all, have been the basis for the Big Book forgiveness concept.

4. Confess your sins one to another. It has often been noted that *both* the Oxford Group concept of sharing by confession *and* Step Five in the Big Book were derived from James 5:16:

> Confess your faults one to another, and pray for one another, that ye may be healed.

Of much more significance than "sharing by confession" and the source of Step Five is the direct patterning of Akron's "real surrenders" on this verse and those surrounding it. Akron brothers did pray for the new man. First, they brought him to Christ; they prayed for him as he accepted Christ and uttered with them his own prayers that alcohol be taken out of his life, that he be cured, and that he be enabled to live by the principles of Christ. The objective was to have him become a Christian—then relying on the power and guidance of God for cure and a life lived in obedience to the cardinal doctrines of Christ.

The Roman Catholic Church had problems with this interpretation of James. It talked irrelevantly and with condemnation about "open confessions" in the Oxford

Group and then relevantly about that church's insistence that confessions be made to a priest—not a group of "elders."

5. Effectual, fervent prayer works. James 5:16 states:

> The effectual fervent prayer of a righteous man availeth much.

A.A.'s Big Book Fourth Edition says:

> Step Eleven suggests prayer and meditation. We shouldn't be shy on this matter of prayer. Better men than we are using it constantly. It works, if we have the proper attitude and work at it.

James 5:16 could well have been a major, albeit unacknowledged, basis for the Big Book comments on the effectiveness of prayer.

6. Anointing with oil and effecting healings achieved through prayer by elders. See James 5:13-16.

One A.A. writer, who was sponsored by the venerable old-timer Clarence Snyder, has repeatedly suggested that, in their "surrenders," early AAs almost literally followed the foregoing verses from James. Many others (seven that I have personally interviewed—Berry W., Grace S., Steve F., John S., Dick B., Dale M., and Jack R.) who also were sponsored by Clarence Snyder, have stated emphatically that this contention is in error. In fact, A.A. old-timer Larry Bauer from Ohio both wrote and phoned me shortly before his death to say that he was quite familiar with the Akron surrenders, that he had been taken upstairs and was there born again, but that there had been *no anointing with oil.*

Before we leave the Book of James, however, several comments should be made about surrenders, the Akron prayers, and the question of anointing.

First, there seems little confirmation of the story by one of Clarence Snyder's sponsees that Dr. Bob, T. Henry Williams, and the Akron pioneers took a newcomer "upstairs," had him "surrender" to Christ, prayed for him and with him, and anointed him with oil. The oil part has simply not been proven to my satisfaction in view of the fact that six of Clarence Snyder's presently living sponsees have told me personally that they knew of no anointing as they were taken through surrenders and later the Steps or nor had they heard history such an account from Clarence.

Second, in preparing my biography of the role of Clarence and his wife Grace in A.A., I spent a week in company with my son Ken at Grace's home at Jacksonville, Florida. And I think it is fair to say that there is nothing about Clarence's ministry and practices that was not covered with Grace (See Dick B., *That Amazing Grace, supra*). Grace talked at length about what Clarence told her about the pioneer program, the surrenders, the prayers "upstairs," and how Clarence had taken people through the Steps for years (Dick B., *That Amazing Grace, supra*, pp. 6, 27). But I can't recall Grace's mentioning anointing with oil by the pioneers though she and Clarence practiced this in their healing work and in the "prayer and praise" segments of their spiritual retreats, after the retreat itself had concluded (See particularly Dick B., *That Amazing Grace, supra*, pp. 95-97, 101, 6, 27). To be sure, many of the elements of the James verses *were* followed by the pioneers including those relating to confession, healing, and prayer.

Third, in his later years, Clarence Snyder had, as we've said, founded and conducted retreats for AAs and their families. Most are still being held. At these retreats, there is a "prayer and praise" session where there *is* anointing with oil and prayer for those in need. The sessions *follow* the close of the retreat itself. See *Our A.A. Legacy to the Faith Community: A Twelve-Step Guide for Those Who Want to Believe*. By Three Clarence Snyder Sponsee Old-timers and Their Wives. Compiled and Edited by Dick B. (FL: Came to Believe Publications, 2005), pp. 99-100.

Finally, we make particular mention of the pioneer confession, prayer, healing, and anointing ideas in James because so many of the healing practices of the Christian church in the beginning and throughout later centuries did rely on the words of St. James and did heal with the laying on of hands and anointing with oil. There is an enormous amount of scholarly writing on

James 5:16, confession, "Unction," prayer by the elders, and the laying on of hands in connection with Christian healing. These writings certainly did not all escape the notice and readings by Dr. Bob on Christian healing.

Probably the leading work on anointing and Scripture is F.W. Puller, *The Anointing of the Sick in Scripture and Tradition, with some Considerations on the Numbering of the Sacraments* (London: Society For Promoting Christian Knowledge, 1904). Others include Percy Dearmer, *Body and Soul: An Enquiry into the Effects of Religion upon Health, with a description of Christian Works of Healing From the New Testament to the Present Day* (London: Sir Isaac Pitman & Sons, Ltd., 1909), 217-255, 287-292, 396-400; J. R. Pridie, *The Church's Ministry of Healing* (London: Society For Promoting Christian Knowledge, 1926), pp. 67-86, 110-114; George Gordon Dawson, *Healing: Pagan and Christian* (London: Society For Promoting Christian Knowledge, 1935), pp. 146-159; John Maillard, *Healing In The Name of Jesus* (London: Hodder & Stoughton, 1936), pp. 116, 283-284; James Moore Hickson, *Heal The Sick* (London: Methuen & Co., Ltd., 1924), pp. 252-269; and Evelyn Frost, *Christian Healing, 2d ed.* (London: A. R. Mowbray & Co., Ltd., 1949), pp. 331-332.

These healing points are also extensively documented and discussed in the titles listed in the bibliographies in my recent works on healing and cure. See Dick B., *Cured: Proven Help for Alcoholics and Addicts* (Kihei, HI: Paradise Research Publications, Inc., 2003); *When Early AAs Were Cured. And Why* (Kihei, HI: Paradise Research Publications, Inc., 2003); and *God and*

Alcoholism: Our Growing Challenge in the 21st Century (Kihei, HI: Paradise Research Publications, Inc., 2002). All the foregoing materials cast a new light on how and why early AAs all said they had been cured; that there was a cure for alcoholism; and that they had developed a cure.

Their belief in healing and cure was supported and fortified by nineteen centuries of Christian healing records.

There is newly confirmed early A.A. history of the bringing of newcomers to Christ, having them ask God to take alcohol out of their lives, and having them ask in Jesus' name for strength and guidance to live by His principles. (See Mitchell K. *How It Worked*. NY: A.A. Big Book Study Group, 1999, pp. 58, 69-71, 139, 215-216; Clarence Snyder, *Going Through the Steps*. FL: Stephen Foreman, 1985); *Three Clarence Snyder Sponsees, Our A.A. Legacy, supra*. There is also newly confirmed proof that Akron old timers prayed for and with the newcomer in their "surrenders"--asking God to heal, guide, and strengthen. There is a vast amount of newly gathered evidence of a decade of early A.A. cures in its first decade of existence. You can find the documentation and accounts of these facts in my titles cited immediately above; in Mitchell K.'s *How It Worked, supra*; and also in several very recent titles by a prodigious writer and careful researcher new to our A.A. historian scene. See Richard K., *Separating Fact From Fiction: How Revisionists Have Led Our History Astray* (Haverhill, MA: Golden Text Publishing Co., 2003); *So You Think Drunks Can't Be Cured?* (Haverhill, MA: Golden Text Publishing Co., 2003).

I believe all the foregoing historical facts are important. The convictions about "healing" and "cure" were so evident and strong in early A.A. And a return of healing emphasis whatever the technique or Biblical authority is urgently needed in today's recovery programs (particularly those being launched in the "faith based community" sector).

What These Historical Facts about A.A. and Its Roots in the Book of James Offer Believers and Others in A.A. Today

If you are going to invent gods, place your faith in meetings, concentrate on not drinking, ignore the need to change your life, fail to ask God's help and guidance, and reject prayers for genuine healing, then just forget the Book of James in A.A. today.

My premise is that the Word of God contains the Will of God. If you don't like the Bible, don't believe in God, don't want to hear about Jesus Christ, think A.A. is supposed to be irreligious, and want the easy way of attendance at meetings often just "centers of self-centeredness," then you don't need James or even the Good Book itself. But James contains some powerful injunctions about walking God's way, rejecting temptation, resisting the tempter, and being cured of any temptation, sickness, and addictive urges.

One misguided, seemingly mean-tempered, moderator (recently deceased) of a couple of history chat groups on-line epitomized (with her censorship ideas) the rigidity which will, if not abandoned, continue to insure sickness, reject cure, and suppress history itself. This moderator told her fans that her web-sites were "safe." She actually banned or deleted contributions from those she thought were "preaching," or departing from some of her time-honored myths, or daring to speak of pioneer reliance on God, study of the Bible, achievement of cure, or Jesus Christ. Sadly, she had begun attracting quite a few "history lovers" to her forums. But her censorial attitude and the tacit approval of her forum bespeak the kind of destructive rigidity many A.A. critics see in the tightly controlled A.A. publications of today.

Principles from the Book of James you can take to the bank. Here are some simple points from James in the Good Book that believers who qualify as "real" alcoholics, and others searching for God's truth, can grab and hold.

Abstain, abstain, abstain: Excessive drinking starts from temptation and is appropriately called in the Bible "sin."

Be patient in your walk with God.

Ask God's wisdom and guidance with unwavering belief in His goodness.

Reject temptation. That is your job. God doesn't tempt, but, according to James, the devil sure does.

Do what God says, don't just listen to the Word and remain passive.

Anger, envy, strife, criticism, and grudges are devilish in origin and results; and they disobey God's Commandments.

Remember that your faith in God's love and power is to be accompanied by deeds consistent with His will.

Remember that your erring tongue can harm and constitute real sinning, and that its utterances—to be appropriate—must be consistent with good works.

Don't complain about unanswered prayers until your prayers coincide with God's will.

Submit yourself to God. Resist the devil. Believe the devil will take a hike.

And he will.

Cleanse your hands.

If you draw near to God, He will draw near to you.

Humility in seeking God, is an essential to His lifting you up.

Openly place your faults on the table and eliminate them.

Ask other believers for their prayers.

Ask God in the name of Jesus Christ for healing and cure and for solutions to all your problems.

Expect and believe for deliverance.

The effectual fervent prayer of a believer pays off.

The Pioneer A.A. program illustrates for us the relevance of James today: As I have written in so many of my publications, the early A.A. program was simple and effective. It produced a high rate of cures that has not been equaled without God. Its basic ideas came, as Dr. Bob declared, from the Bible itself. The early program still offers these choices to anyone in A.A. today:

You either want to quit, to resist temptation, and to do what it takes; or you don't.

You either will abstain from drinking; resist temptation; and quit for good; or you won't.

[Yes! It is a matter of choice. It's your choice.]

You will seek medical help at the beginning if needed; or you won't.

You will accept Jesus Christ as the way, and the only way, to come to the Creator; or you won't.

You will ask our Yahweh our Creator, in the name of Jesus Christ, for healing, for strength, for guidance, for forgiveness, and for help in your daily walk in reliance on, and obedience to, Him; or you won't.

You will recognize that the Bible, the messages revealed by God to believers when He chooses (and they seek His guidance); and renewing of your mind with what God tells us are each of the three keys to obeying God and receiving His promises. You either believe this, or you don't.

A Key from James that should be a major factor for believers in A.A. today: You should make every

effort to recognize that the key to the early A.A. program was not drunkalogs. It was not meetings. It was not cleaning up a drunk. It was Christian fellowship and witnessing by those who had suffered from similar problems, by those who had followed the path known as the "way," by those who had been cured themselves, and by those who therefore were able to describe exactly how it had happened, what they had done, and how God had done for them what they could not do for themselves.

This process involved an understanding of several factors: The malady, the requirement of abstaining from temptation, the necessity for Christ, the promises of God, the power of God, and the necessity for obedience to God's will. And all had been covered in the Good Book and known for centuries before A.A.

The malady-drunkenness:

> Proverbs 23:29-35: "Who hath woe? . . . . They that tarry too long at the wine. . . . At the last it biteth like a serpent, and stingeth like an adder. . . ."

Proverbs 31:4-6: "It is not for kings, O Lemuel, it is not for kings to drink wine; nor for princes strong drink: Lest they drink, and forget the law, and pervert the judgment of any of the afflicted. . . ."

Galatians 5:19-21: "Now the works of the flesh are manifest. . . envyings, murders, drunkenness. . . . they which do such things shall not inherit the kingdom of God."

Ephesians 5:18: "And be not drunk with wine, wherein is excess. . . .

The solution-submission to God and resisting the devil:

James 4:7-10: "Submit yourselves therefore to God. Resist the devil, and he will flee from you. . . . Cleanse your hands, ye sinners; and purify your hearts, ye double minded. . . . Humble yourselves in the sight of the Lord, and he shall lift you up."

The necessity for Christ and reliance on the promises of God:

Acts 4:10-12: "Be it known to you all, and to all the people of Israel, that by the name of Jesus Christ of Nazareth, whom you crucified, whom God raised from the dead, even by him doth this man [the man previously lame from birth] stand here before you whole. . . . Neither is there salvation in any other; for there is none other name under heaven given among men, whereby we must be saved."

Acts 2:38-39: ". . . Repent, and be baptized every one of you in the name of Jesus Christ for the remission of sins, and ye shall receive the gift of the Holy Ghost. For the promise is unto you and to your children, and to all that are afar off, even as many as the Lord our God shall call."

Acts 2:1-9: "Now Peter and John went up together unto the temple at the hour of prayer, being the ninth hour. And a certain man lame from his mother's womb was carried, whom they laid daily at the gate of the temple which is called Beautiful, to ask alms of them that entered into the temple. Who seeing Peter and John about to go into the temple asked an alms. And Peter, fastening his eyes upon him with John, said, Look on us. And he gave heed unto them, expecting to receive something of them. Then Peter said, Silver and gold have I none; but such as I have give I thee: In the name of Jesus Christ of Nazareth rise up and walk. And he took him by the right hand, and lifted him up: and immediately his feet and ankle bones received strength. And he leaping up stood, and walked, and entered into the temple, walking, and leaping, and praising God: And all the people saw him walking and praising God."

The Power of God:

Ephesians 1:19: "And what is the exceeding greatness of his power to us- ward who believe, according to the working of his mighty power."

Obedience to God's will—walking in the Spirit, obeying unto righteousness, enduring temptation and resisting it, and keeping God's commandments:

Galatians 5:16: "This I say then, Walk in the Spirit, and ye shall not fulfill the lust of the flesh." [A choice!]

Romans 6:16: "Know ye not, that to whom ye yield yourselves servants to obey, his servants are ye to whom ye obey, whether of sin unto death or obedience unto righteousness." [A choice!]

James 1:12-16: "Blessed is the man that endureth temptation: for when he is tried, he shall receive the crown of life which the Lord hath promised to them that love him. . . . But every man is tempted, when he is drawn way of his own lust, and enticed. Then when lust hath conceived, it bringeth forth sin: and sin, when it is finished, bringeth forth death. Do not err, my beloved brethren." [A choice!]

Ecclesiastes 12:13: "Let us hear the conclusion of the whole matter: Fear God, and keep his commandments: for this is the whole duty of man." [A choice]

What God has really made available to obedient believers:

I found, for my cure, that the promises of God were backed by the willingness and ability of Yahweh the Creator to perform them. Until I dug into the Good

Book, read it frequently, renewed my mind with its contents, prayed for help as it instructs, and believed God, no cure occurred. Once I did turn to the Good Book and do the suggested, my cure was received.

Cure for me certainly means at the least wholeness. From my first day in A.A., I have never picked up a drink or taken a sleeping pill. That part, with God's help, was easy for me though it may not be for some others. But that was neither cure nor wholeness.

The tough part meant dealing with two major elements of the spiritual malady:

> 1. Awaiting an end to severe acute and delayed withdrawal accompanied by seizures, delirium, confusion, forgetfulness, insomnia, shaking, depression, and dependence upon others.

> **2.** Enduring seemingly hopeless despair, anxiety, guilt, shame, and terror factors certainly arising from my own past behavior, endless legal problems, and prospects of punishments. These were the biggies.

The withdrawal, both acute and delayed, faded away with time and sobriety. But I overcame the biggies only by placing my trust in God, believing what His Word told me about the solutions, holding His words in my mind, and walking out in reliance on them:

> I had to believe and act on Proverbs 29:25, which declared that "The fear of man bringeth a

snare, but whoso putteth his trust in the Lord shall be safe." Unceasing terror did have me entrapped. I then did put my trust in Yahweh, the Lord; and I was cured of the terror and found myself safe in all the tribulations I had been terrified of dealing with.

I had to believe and act on Philippians 4:6-7, which declared: "Be careful [anxious] for nothing; but in everything by prayer and supplication with thanksgiving let your request be made known to God. And the peace of God, which passeth all understanding, shall keep your hearts and minds through Christ Jesus." I had become so filled with anxiety that I shook all over; but as I held these verses in mind, asked God for help, thanking Him in the name of Jesus Christ, the anxiety left, and the peace to deal with things took its place.

My guilt and shame over the things I had done while drinking were overcome when I saw the love that God had shed on me when I accepted and stood on what His son had done. Romans 5:1 assured me: "Therefore being justified [acquitted] by faith, we have peace with God through our Lord Jesus Christ." Romans 5:8 said: "But God commendeth his love toward us in that, while we were yet sinners, Christ died for us." Romans 8:1 confirmed: "There is therefore now no condemnation to them which are in Christ Jesus. . ." And then there was Ephesians 1:4: "According as he hath chosen us in him before the foundation of the world, that we should be holy and without blame before him in love."

These Biblical affirmations of our righteousness and real standing as sons of God may baffle many who deal with alcoholics. Thus they baffled a psychiatrist like mine who began treating me in the earliest days by examining guilt in depth. They baffled a naïve sponsor like mine who thought, bless his heart, a Fifth Step confession would wipe away sins. But each these well-meaning people left me with deep guilt and shame—one declaring it was OK, and the other telling me that he also had such guilt and shame as well.

For me, however, there was no release until I understood the Grace of God. I had accepted His son believed in the righteousness and justification I had received as a gift, not through therapy or confession. This remission of sins past and my redemption were truths which I believed and which truly *made* me free. That was wholeness.

There had also been that yawning, threatening despair which seemed to block any future wholeness and joy and leave me falling deeper into a dark hole. But I found and believed Psalm 31:1: "In thee, O Lord, do I put my trust; let me never be ashamed: deliver me in thy righteousness. . . . Pull me out of the net that they have laid privily for me: for thou art my strength. Into thine hand I commit my spirit: thou hast redeemed me, O Lord God of truth." I took to be true the words of Psalm 34:6: "This poor man cried, and the Lord heard him, and saved him out of all his troubles." I know how hard it was for me and is for others to believe that seemingly hopeless circumstances can and will be overcome when reliance is placed on the

Creator. But they were for me.   That was wholeness.

I took great comfort from the declaration that Anne Smith included in her journal and which came from 3 John 2: "Beloved, I wish above all things that thou mayest prosper and be in health, even as thy soul prospereth." This verity is what I thought of when I heard AAs say: "Let go, and Let God." I believed and still believe that God does not want us in a pit. God can and did literally and figuratively pull me out of the net once I put my mind on what God could do and what Jesus Christ had accomplished, rather than on what others and I thought it was impossible to do.

That, I found, was also a characteristic of some of the earliest A.A. thinking. It exemplified the needed believing, when Ebby Thacher, Rev. Sam Shoemaker, and then Bill Wilson all declared that God can and will do for us what we cannot do for ourselves. That's one of the Big Book promises also! It's not conditioned on "faith without works is dead." It's about believing what God tells you can be done. Look at the story of Jesus' rebuking the deaf and dumb spirit and commanding that it leave the child and enter him no more. Jesus had said to the father: "If thou canst believe, all things are possible to him that believeth." And (says the Bible) "And straightaway the father of the child cried out, and said with tears, Lord, I believe; help thou mine unbelief." (See Mark 9:17-29).

The promise implied in 3 John 2 has become a reality: "Beloved, I wish above all things that thou mayest prosper and be in health, even as thy soul prospereth."

Dr. Bob's wife, Anne Smith, elatedly put that verse in the journal that she shared with early AAs and their families. It probably exemplifies a large chunk of the cure God provides to those who believe. It is wholeness.

After 15 years of research into early A.A., I firmly believe that, over nineteen years ago, I began in A.A. pursuing the pioneers' path, though I did not originally know they had trod that path with astonishing success. And I can today understand how and why the Book of James was such a favored guide for them. In fact, what a different and successful A.A. it would be if one or more meetings were devoted to reading and re-reading the Book of James hopefully in company with this study and believing without wavering that healing and cure can and do result when the Good Book (and Dr. Bob's "absolutely essential" Sermon on the Mount, 1 Corinthians 13, and the Book of James) is studied, learned, and believed. That worked in the first decade for the pioneers, and it can work for those today who "really try" and do, and who embrace the path that leads to abstinence, prosperity, health, an abundant life, and everlasting life. That's wholeness.

Part Two:

The Sermon on the Mount in A.A.

One of the Three Parts of the Bible Early AAs Considered Essential

The "Sermon"—What it is, and What People Say About it

When I was a kid, my Uncle Gene used to say that his "religion" was the "Sermon on the Mount." I know that Uncle Gene didn't belong to a church and never attended a church service except an Easter Sunrise Service once a year. He never mentioned the Bible, and I'm pretty sure he never read it. I'm not sure he had any idea that Jesus was connected with the sermon. At least he never mentioned Jesus. Yet he thought the "Sermon on the Mount" was the cat's pajamas.

My first grand-sponsor in A.A. used to suggest that the men he sponsored read "the Sermon on the Mount." Turned out, he had suggested Emmet Fox's book—something I learned when I saw that several of the men had Fox's book and said it had been recommended by my grand-sponsor. Later, at our Wednesday night meeting, this man said the "Sermon on the Mount" and the Bible were very special in A.A. But he later confided to me that he had never read the Bible. On several other occasions, he warned men that AAs who read the Bible got drunk and that they should have been reading the Big Book and nothing else. My own first sponsor told me the same things. Together, these men tried to

73

stop me from taking my sponsees to a Bible fellowship. Both talked lots about their "higher power," a little about Fox's "sermon," but never mentioned Jesus Christ in my presence.

I had an A.A. friend come up to me one day and ask me where the "Lord's Prayer" came from. He wanted to know where he could find it. Of course, he had been saying it at the end of every A.A. meeting every day for months and months. He had expressed interest in going to a Bible fellowship, and it's just possible he put together the idea that the Lord's Prayer and the Bible were somehow related.

As to my own knowledge about the "sermon," I have to confess that, even though my mother studied the Bible daily, wrote me about it frequently, and used to read to me from the Psalms when I was ill, I don't think I knew very much about the sermon. I think I believed that Jesus had delivered the talk to his disciples on a mountain. Also, I had heard stuff about the "Beatitudes," the "Lord's Prayer," "turn the other cheek," "love your enemies," and the "Golden Rule." But I had never heard of, or used, a Bible Concordance. And I am sure I couldn't have found those verses or sayings in the Bible to save my soul!

Early AAs Heard about It All the Time

The Sermon on the Mount had a different history in early A.A. Both Bill Wilson and Dr. Bob said several times that Jesus' Sermon on the Mount contained the underlying philosophy of A.A. A.A.'s own literature reports: "He [Dr. Bob] cited the Sermon on the Mount as containing the underlying spiritual philosophy of

A.A." (*DR. BOB and the Good Oldtimers*. NY: Alcoholics Anonymous World Services, Inc., 1980, p. 228). Dr. Bob had no hesitancy about reading from the Bible and reading this Sermon from it at meetings. An A.A. *Grapevine* article states that at a meeting led by Dr. Bob, Dr. Bob "put his foot on the rung of a dining-room chair, identified himself as an alcoholic, and began reading the Sermon on the Mount" (*DR. BOB, supra*, p. 218). Dr. Bob pointed out that there were no twelve steps at the beginning, that "our stories didn't amount to anything to speak of," and that they [A.A.'s "older ones"] were "convinced that the answer to their problems was in the Good Book" (*DR. BOB, supra*, p. 96).

A.A. Old-timer Clarence Snyder pointed out as to Dr. Bob: "If someone asked him a question about the program, his usual response was: 'What does it say in the Good Book?'" (*DR. BOB, supra*, p. 144). Bob said quite clearly: "I didn't write the Twelve Steps. I had nothing to do with the writing of them" but that "We already had the basic ideas, though not in terse and tangible form. We got them as a result of our study of the Good Book" (*DR. BOB, supra*, pp. 96-97). Dr. Bob stressed over and over that the "the parts we found absolutely essential were" the Book of James, the Sermon on the Mount, and 1 Corinthians 13 *(e.g. DR. BOB, supra,* p. 96). In the Foreword Dr. Bob's son "Smitty" wrote for my book, *The Good Book and The Big Book*, "Smitty" pointed to the importance in A.A. of James, the Sermon, and Corinthians; and I heard Smitty repeat his statement at several large A.A. history meetings, including one at A.A.'s San Diego International Convention in 1995. Dr. Bob's sponsee Clarence Snyder, got sober in February of 1938 and later became the AA with the greatest amount of sobriety. Clarence often echoed Dr. Bob's words about the Bible and the three essential parts. Also, in a talk given to AAs in Glenarden, Maryland, on August 8, 1981, Clarence said: "This program emanates from the Sermon on the Mount and the Book of James. If you want to know where this program came from, read the fifth, sixth, seventh chapters of Matthew. Study it over and over, and you'll see the whole program in there" (Glen Cove, NY: Glenn K. Audio Tape #2451).

Of course, the Lord's Prayer itself can be found in several of the Gospels and particularly in Jesus' sermon at Matthew 6:9-13. This prayer from the sermon was originally and frequently recited by the A.A. pioneers at the close of every meeting (*e.g.: DR. BOB, supra*, pp. 141, 148, 183, 261)—just as it was in the meetings of the Oxford Group, from which A.A. derived. And just as it still is in most A.A. meetings today.

Bill Wilson actually quoted from two parts of the sermon in the Big Book—though he never indicated his source. He borrowed the phrase "Thy will be done" [from Matthew 6:10] and partly quoted "Thou shalt love thy neighbor as thyself" from Matthew 5:43 (also found in many other places in the Bible—*e.g.*: Leviticus 19:18; Romans 13:9; Galatians 5:14; James 2:8).

Dr. Bob read and circulated among early AAs and their families a good many materials that discussed every facet of the Sermon—*e.g.: Studies in the Sermon on the Mount* by Oswald Chambers (London: Simpkin, Marshall, Ltd., n.d.); *The Christ of the Mount: A Working Philosophy of Life* by E. Stanley Jones (NY: The Abingdon Press, 1931); *The Sermon on the Mount* by

Emmet Fox (NY: Harper & Row, 1934); *The Lord's Prayer and Other Talks on Prayer from The Camps Farthest Out* by Glenn Clark (MN: Macalester Park Publishing Co., 1932); and *I Will Lift Up Mine Eyes* by Glenn Clark (NY: Harper & Brothers, 1937). See Dick B. *Dr. Bob and His Library*, 3rd ed. (Kihei, HI: Paradise Research Publications, Inc., 1998); *DR. BOB and the Good Oldtimers, supra*, pp.310-311.

Many Oxford Group books discussed the sermon as did many of the daily devotionals the early AAs used—devotionals such as *The Upper Room* and *The Runner's Bible*. See DR. BOB, supra, pp. 71, 139, 151, 178, 220, 311 and, as to *The Runner's Bible, DR. BOB, supra*, p. 293; *RHS*. NY: A.A. Grapevine, Inc., 1951, p. 34; Dick B., *Good Morning*, 2d ed., *Dr. Bob and His Library*, 3rd ed., and *The Books Early AAs Read for Spiritual Growth*, 7th ed.

A Study of the Actual Sermon on the Mount AAs Read

(Matthew Chapters 5-7)

This discussion will not deal with a particular book or commentary on Matthew chapters 5-7. It will focus on the verses in the Sermon on the Mount itself. For this Sermon, which Jesus delivered, was not the property of some present-day commentator or writer. The fact that Dr. Bob read the Matthew chapters *themselves,* as well as many interpretations of them, verifies the A.A. belief that the Sermon was one of the principles comprising Athe common property of mankind, which Bill Wilson said the AAs had borrowed. And here are some major points that appear to have found their way from the Sermon into the basic ideas of the Big Book. The points were, of course, in the Sermon itself. In addition, the pioneers read many books and articles on and about the sermon which are thoroughly documented in my title, *The Good Book and The Big Book: A.A.'s Roots in the Bible.* Those items further illustrate some of the points made in the Sermon and that might have found their way into A.A.

The Lord's Prayer Matthew 6:9-13

Oxford Group meetings closed with the Lord's Prayer in New York and in Akron. In early A.A., the alcoholics also closed meetings with the Lord's Prayer. Moreover, I have personally attended at least two thousand A.A. meetings, and almost every one has closed with the Lord's Prayer. At the 1990 International A.A. Conference in Seattle, which was a first for me, some 50,000 members of Alcoholics Anonymous joined in closing their meetings with the Lord's Prayer. The question here concerns what parts, if any, of the Lord's Prayer found their way into the Big Book, Twelve Steps, A.A. Slogans, and the A.A. fellowship; and we hasten to remind the reader that the prayer is *part of the Sermon on the Mount.*

Here are the verses of the Lord's Prayer (*King James Version*) as found in Matt. 6:9-13. Jesus instructed the Judeans, After this manner therefore pray ye:

> Our Father which art in heaven, Hallowed be thy name.
> Thy kingdom come. Thy will be done in earth, as *it is* in heaven. Give us this day our daily bread.
> And forgive us our debts, as we forgive our

debtors.
And lead us not into temptation, but deliver us from evil: For thine is the kingdom, and the power, and the glory, for ever. Amen.

Dr. Bob studied specific commentaries on the Sermon by Oswald Chambers, Glenn Clark, Emmet Fox, and E. Stanley Jones. And these writers extracted a good many teachings, prayer guides, and theological ideas from Lord's Prayer verses in the Sermon. But there are a few concepts and phrases in the Lord's Prayer itself which either epitomize A.A. thinking or can be found in its language whether or not the A.A. traces came from the Lord's Prayer or from other portions of the Bible. For example, the Big Book uses the word Father when referring to the Creator Yahweh, our God; and the context shows that this usage and name came from the Bible. The Oxford Group also used the term Father, among other names, when referring to God. The concept and expression of God as Father is not confined to the Sermon on the Mount. It can be found in many other parts of the New Testament. But AAs have given the Our Father prayer a special place in their meetings. Thus the Lord's Prayer seems the likely source of their use of the word Father.

The phrase Thy will be done is directly quoted, or is the specific subject of reference, in the Big Book several times (Big Book, 4th ed., pp. 63, 67, 76, 85, 88). It underlies A.A.'s oft-mentioned contrast between self-will and God's will. The Oxford Group stressed, as do A.A.'s Third and Seventh Step prayers, that there must be a *decision to do God's will and surrender to His will.* These ideas were also symbolized in the A.A. prayer's Thy will be done.

Finally, "Forgive us our "debts" or trespasses certainly states that God can and will forgive; and these concepts can be found in the Big Book, whether they came from the Lord's Prayer or from other important Biblical sources such as the Book of James (James 5:16), the writings of Paul in Colossians 3:13, and 1 John 1:9.

The Full ᴀSermon on the Mount: Matthew Chapters 5-7

Dr. Bob studied, and circulated among early AAs, an E. Stanley Jones book, *The Christ of the Mount* (Nashville: Abingdon, 1931; Festival ed., 1985, pp. 36-37) which outlined the Sermon's contents in this fashion:

1. The goal of life: To be perfect or complete as the Father in heaven is perfect or complete (5:48); with twenty-seven marks of this perfect life (5:1-47).

2. [Jones wrote of these verses:] The perfect life consists in being poor in spirit, in mourning, in being meek, in hungering and thirsting after righteousness, in being merciful, pure in heart, in being a peacemaker, persecuted for righteousness sake and yet rejoicing and being exceeding glad, in being the salt of the earth, the light of the world, having a righteousness that exceeds, in being devoid of anger with the brother, using no contemptuous words, allowing no one to hold anything against one, having the spirit of quick agreement, no inward lustful thinking, relentless against anything that offends against the highest, right relations in the home life, truth in speech and attitude, turning the other cheek, giving the cloak also, going the second mile, giving to those

who ask and from those who would borrow turning not away, loving even one's enemies, praying for those that persecute (pp. 50-51).

3. A diagnosis of the reason why men do not reach or move on to that goal: Divided personality (6:1-6; 7:1-6).

4. The Divine offer of an adequate moral and spiritual re-enforcement so that men can move on to that goal: The Holy Spirit to them that ask him (7:7-11).

5. After making the Divine offer he gathers up and emphasizes in two sentences our part in reaching that goal. Toward others we are to do unto others as we would that they should do unto us (7:12); toward ourselves we are to lose ourselves by entering the straight gate (7:13).

6. The test of whether we are moving on to that goal, or whether this Divine Life is operative within us: By their fruits (7:15-23).

7. The survival value of this new life and the lack of survival value of life lived in any other way: The house founded on rock and the house founded on sand (7:24-27).

Our own discussion will review Jesus' Sermon, chapter by chapter. It will pinpoint some principal thoughts that Dr. Bob and Bill may have had in mind when they each said that the Sermon on the Mount contained the underlying philosophy of Alcoholics Anonymous. Here follows our review:

Matthew Chapter 5

1. The Beatitudes. The Beatitudes are found in Matt. 5:3-11. The word beatitudes refers to the first word Blessed in each of these verses. Merriam Webster's says blessed means enjoying the bliss of heaven. The word in the Greek New Testament from which blessed was translated means, happy, according Biblical scholar Ethelbert Bullinger. *Vine's Expository Dictionary of Old and New Testament Words* explains the word Blessed as follows: In the beatitudes the Lord indicates not only the characters that are blessed, but the nature of that which is the highest good. Dr. Bob's wife Anne Smith described the Beatitudes in the Sermon on the Mount as Athe Christ-like virtues to be cultivated (Dick B., *Anne Smith's Journal*, p. 135).

The beatitude verses can be found at the very beginning of Jesus's sermon and read as follows:

And seeing the multitudes, he went up into a mountain: and when he was set, his disciples came unto him:
And he opened his mouth, and taught them, saying,
Blessed are the poor in spirit: for theirs is the kingdom of heaven.
Blessed are they that mourn: for they shall be comforted.
Blessed are the meek: for they shall inherit the earth.
Blessed are they which do hunger and thirst after righteousness: for they shall be filled.
Blessed are the merciful: for they shall obtain mercy.
Blessed are the pure in heart: for they shall see God.
Blessed are the peacemakers: for they shall be

called the children of God.

Blessed are they which are persecuted for righteousness' sake: for theirs is the kingdom of heaven.

Blessed are ye, when men shall revile you, and persecute you, and shall say all manner of evil against you falsely, for my sake.

Rejoice, and be exceeding glad: for great is your reward in heaven: for so persecuted they the prophets which were before you (Matt. 5:1-12)

Italicized below are *Webster's* definitions for the key words in each beatitude verse. Included also are quotes from the *King James Version*, which was the version Dr. Bob and early AAs most used. As the verses appear in the King James, they state: Blessed are:

- the poor *(humble)* in spirit [renouncing themselves, wrote E. Stanley Jones]: for theirs is the kingdom of heaven (v. 3) ;

- they that mourn *(feel or express grief or sorrow):* for they shall be comforted (v. 4);

- the meek *(enduring injury with patience and without resentment);* for they shall inherit the earth (v. 5);

- they which do hunger and thirst after righteousness *(acting in accord with divine or moral law):* for they shall be filled (v. 6);

- the merciful *(compassionate):* for they shall obtain mercy (v. 7);

- the pure *(spotless, stainless)* in heart
  [has a passion for righteousness and a
  compassion for men seeks law and shows
  love, wrote Jones]: for they shall see God
  (v. 8);

- the peacemakers: for they shall be called
  the children of God (v. 9);

- they which are persecuted for
  righteousness sake: for theirs is the
  kingdom of heaven (v. 10);

- ye when men shall revile you, and
  persecute you, and shall say all manner
  of evil against you falsely, for my sake
  (end or purpose): for great is your
  reward in heaven: for so persecuted they
  the prophets which were before you (v.
  11).

Did Dr. Bob, Anne, Bill, or Henrietta Seiberling study
and draw specifically on these beatitude verses as they
put together A.A.'s Akron recovery program? The
author can neither provide nor document any answer.
But there are some ideas common to A.A.'s spiritual
principles in the beatitudes as you see them expressed
above. These are:

(1) Humility overcoming self;

(2) Comfort for the suffering;

(3) Patience and tolerance to the end of
eliminating resentment;

(4) Harmonizing one's actions with God's will;

(5) Compassion, which *Webster* defines as sympathetic consciousness of others distress together with a desire to alleviate;

(6) Cleaning houseBwhich means seeking obedience to God and, based on the principles of love, straightening out harms caused by disobedience;

(7) Making peace;

(8) Standing for and acting upon spiritual principles, whatever the cost, because they are God's principles.

The foregoing are Twelve Step ideas that can be found in the Beatitudes; and A.A. founders probably saw them there as well they can most certainly be found in the Big Book. Thus the Big Book frequently emphasizes humility, comforting others, patience and tolerance, AThy will be done, compassion, amends, peacemaking, emulating these as Acardinal principles of Jesus Christ which Anne Smith suggested were Christ-like virtues to be cultivated.

2.   Letting your light shine. Matt. 5:13-16 suggest glorifying your Heavenly Father by letting others *see* your good works in practice. That is, Letting your light shine does not mean glorifying yourself, but rather glorifying God by letting others see your spiritual walk *in action* see the immediate results of your surrender to the Master. These ideas may be reflected in the Big Book's statement: Our real purpose is to fit ourselves to be of maximum service to God. . . . (p. 77).

3. Obeying the Ten Commandments. In Matt. 5:17-21, Jesus reiterates the importance of obeying the law and the prophets, specifically referring to Exod. 20:13 (Thou shalt not kill), but obviously referring as well to the other important commandments such as having no other god but Yahweh (Exod. 20:2-3), worshiping no other god (Exod. 20:4-5), eschewing adultery (Exod. 20:14), refraining from stealing (Exod. 20:15), and so on. And even though some of these commandments may have fallen between the cracks in today's A.A., they very clearly governed the moral standards of early A.A. that Dr. Bob and the Akron AAs embraced. The Ten Commandments were part of early A.A. pamphlets and literature, and (for example) Dr. Bob and the Akron AAs would have nothing to do with a man who was committing adultery (See *DR. BOB*, *supra*, p. 131 – Item Number 3).

4. The Law of Love in action. In Matt. 5:17-47, Jesus confirms that the Law of Love fulfills the Old Testament Law. He rejects anger without cause, unresolved wrongs to a brother, quibbling with an adversary, lust and impurity, adultery, retaliation, and hatred of an enemy. The author's title *The Oxford Group & Alcoholics Anonymous* covers many of these ideas as roots of A.A. principles. And such materials in these verses in Matthew may very well have influenced A.A. language about:

(a) *Overcoming resentments*—Matthew 5:22:

. . . I say unto you, That whosoever is angry with his brother without a cause shall be in danger of the judgment. . ." *See Alcoholics Anonymous* 4th ed., p. 67: "God save me from being angry."

(b) *Making restitution*—Matthew 5:23-24:

"Therefore if thou bring thy gift before the altar, and there rememberest that thy brother hath ought against thee; Leave there thy gift before the altar, and go thy way; first be reconciled to thy brother, and then come and offer thy gift;" See *DR. BOB*, *supra*, p. 308: "We learned what was meant when Christ said, "Therefore if thou bring thy gift to the altar. . . "

(c) *Avoidance of retaliation for wrongdoing by others*—Matthew 5:38-39:

'Ye have heard that it hath been said, An eye for an eye, and a tooth for a tooth: But I say unto you, That ye resist not evil: but whosoever shall smite thee on thy right cheek, turn to him the other also; See *Alcoholics Anonymous*, 4th ed., p. 67: "Though we did not like their symptoms and the way these disturbed us. . . . We avoid retaliation or argument. . . . at least God will show us how to take a kindly and tolerant view of each and every one."

(d) *Making peace with our enemies*—Matthew 5:43-44:

"Ye have heard that it hath been said, Thou shalt love thy neighbor, and hate thine enemy. But I say unto you. Love your enemies, bless them that curse you, do good to them that hate you, and pray for them which despitefully use you, and persecute you." See *Alcoholics Anonymous*, 4th ed., pp. 67, 70: "When a person offended we said to ourselves, "This is a sick man. How can I be helpful to him? . . . Thy will be done. . . . We have begun to learn tolerance, patience, and good will toward all men, even our enemies, for we look on them as sick people."

Matthew Chapter 6

1. **Anonymity**. Matt. 6:1-8, 16-18—urge almsgiving in secret,   praying in secret, fasting in secret, and avoiding vain repetitions, and hypocrisy. These verses could very possibly have played a role in the development of A.A.'s spiritual principle of anonymity. Jesus said, your Father knoweth what things ye have need of, before ye ask him and Athy Father, which seeth in secret, shall reward thee openly. The vain practices which Jesus condemned were acts focusing on self-importance, inflating the ego, and manifesting self-centeredness-- something A.A. disdains. Making a public display of gift-giving, praying, fasting, and repetitive prayers was something Jesus criticized because *of* the pointless hypocrisy of showing off one's feigned piety to men whereas the almsgiving, fasting, and prayers were really addressed to or for or in worship of God, Who already knew the heart of the hypocrite. *See Alcoholics Anonymous*,   4th   ed.,   p.   62:   "Selfishness—self-centeredness! That, we think, is the root of our troubles. . . . Above everything, we alcoholics must be rid of this selfishness." Early Oxford Group and A.A. literature often spoke of God-sufficiency versus self-sufficiency, and "God-centeredness versus self-centeredness. We have located no direct tie between Jesus' teachings on anonymity and A.A.'s Traditions on this principle. But the concepts are parallel; and *The Runner's Bible,* and other A.A. biblical sources that AAs studied, do discuss their significance at some length. Also, see *Alcoholics Anonymous*, 4th ed., pp. 76, 77, 93:

> Our real purpose is to fit ourselves to be of
> maximum service to God and the people around
> us. . . . We will lose interest in selfish things

and gain interest in our fellows. Self-seeking will slip away. . . . To be vital, faith must be accompanied by self-sacrifice and unselfish, constructive action.

2. Forgiveness. Matt. 6:14-15 refer to forgiving men their trespasses; and Emmet Fox's forceful writing about these verses exemplifies the A.A. amends process. Fox said:

> The forgiveness of sins is the central problem of life. . . . It is, of course, rooted in selfishness. . . . We must positively and definitely extend forgiveness to everyone to whom it is possible that we can owe forgiveness, namely, to anyone who we think can have injured us in any way. . . When you hold resentment against anyone, you are bound to that person by a cosmic link, a real, tough metal chain. You are tied by a cosmic tie to the thing that you hate. The one person perhaps in the whole world whom you most dislike is the very one to whom you are attaching yourself by a hook that is stronger than steel (Fox, *The Sermon on the Mount,* pp. 183-88).

There is no assurance that Fox's writing on the sermon's forgiveness point specifically influenced the Big Book's emphasis on forgiveness. To be sure, at least two A.A. history writers have claimed that Fox's writings did influence Bill Wilson. However, other books that were read by early AAs books by such authors as Henry Drummond, Glenn Clark, E. Stanley Jones, and Harry Emerson Fosdick used language similar to that used by Fox in his discussion of forgiveness of enemies. And Jesus' Sermon on the Mount is not the only place in the New Testament where forgiveness is stressed. Thus, after, and even though, Christ had accomplished remission of past sins of believers, Paul wrote:

> Forbearing one another, and forgiving one another, if any man have a quarrel against any: even as Christ forgave you, so also *do ye* (Col. 3:13)

See also the following verse, a favorite often quoted and used by Henrietta Seiberling the well known early A.A. teacher who was often thought of as an A.A. founder:

> If a man say I love God, and hateth his brother. he is a liar: for he that loveth not his brother whom he hath seen, how can he love God whom he hath not seen? (1 John 4:20)

In any event, the Big Book, Fourth Edition, states at page 77:

> The question of how to approach the man we hated will arise. It may be he has done us more harm than we have done him and, though we may have acquired a better attitude toward him, we are still not too keen about admitting our faults. Nevertheless, with a person we dislike, we take the bit in our teeth. It is harder to go to an enemy than to a friend, but we find it more beneficial to us. We go to him in a helpful *and forgiving spirit,* confessing our former ill feeling and expressing our regret. Under no condition do we criticize such a person or argue. Simply we tell him that we will never get over drinking until we have done our utmost

to straighten out the past (italics added). [Note that Wilson makes no effort to argue for forgiveness because of Biblical authority]

3. The sunlight of the Spirit? Speaking of the futility and unhappiness in a life which includes deep resentment, the Big Book states: ʌwhen harboring such feelings we shut ourselves off from the sunlight of the Spirit. One often hears this ʌsunlight expression quoted in A.A. meetings. Yet its origins seem unreported and undocumented. Anne Smith referred frequently in her journal to the verses in 1 John which had to do with fellowship with God and walking in the light as God is light. So did A.A.'s Oxford Group sources. And the following are the most frequently quoted verses from 1 John having to do with God as light and the importance of walking in the light (rather than walking in darkness) in order to have fellowship with Him:

That which we have seen and heard declare we unto you, that ye may have fellowship with us: and truly our fellowship *is* with the Father, and with his Son, Jesus Christ.
And these things write we unto you, that your joy may be full.
This then is the message which we have heard of him, and declare unto you, that God is light, and in him is no darkness at all.
If we say that we have fellowship with him, and walk in darkness, we lie, and do not the truth:
But if we walk in the light, as he is in the light, we have fellowship one with another, and the blood of Jesus Christ his Son cleanseth us from all sin (1 John 1:3-7).

Though this particular discussion is concerned with the Sermon on the Mount, we have mentioned also the foregoing verses from 1 John 1:3-7 (having to do with walking in God's light as against opposed to walking in darkness). For very possibly those ideas in 1 John, together with the following verses in the Sermon, may have given rise to Bill's references to the alcoholic's being blocked from the sunlight of the Spirit when he or she dwells in such dark realms as fear and excessive anger. Matt. 6:22-24 (in the Sermon) state:

> The light of the body is the eye: if therefore thine eye be single, thy whole body shall be full of light.
> But if thine eye be evil, thy whole body shall be full of darkness. If therefore the light that is in thee be darkness, how great *is* that darkness!
> No man can serve two masters: for either he will hate the one, and love the other: or else he will hold to the one, and despise the other. Ye cannot serve God and mammon.

4. Seek ye first the kingdom of God. Matt. 6:24-34 seem to have had tremendous influence on A.A. At least on early A.A.! The substance of these verses is that man will be taken care of when he seeks *first* the kingdom of God and His righteousness. Verse 33 says:

> But seek ye first the kingdom of God, and his righteousness; and all these things [food, clothing, and shelter] shall be added unto you.

Dr. Bob specifically explained the origin of our A.A. slogans Easy Does It and First Things First. *(DR. BOB and the Good Oldtimers,* pp 135, 144, 192, 282). When he was asked the meaning of First Things First, Dr. Bob replied. Seek ye first the kingdom of God and His righteousness, and all these things shall be added unto you. He told his sponsee Clarence Snyder that First Things First came from Matt. 6:33 in the Sermon on the Mount (*DR. BOB, su*pra, p. 144). And this verse was widely quoted in the books that Dr. Bob and the Akron AAs read and recommended (Dick B., *The Good Book and The Big Book,* p. 125, n.119; *That Amazing Grace*, pp. 30, 38).

On page 60, the Big Book states the A.A. solution for relief from alcoholism: AGod could and would if He were *sought.* (italics added). This concept is one of seeking results by reliance on God instead of reliance on self. And this is a bedrock idea in the Big Book. *See Alcoholics Anonymous,* 4th ed., pp. 11, 14, 25, 28, 43, 52-53, 57, 62. In view of Dr. Bob's explanations as to the origin of First Things First, the Big Book's emphasis on seeking very likely came from the seeking the kingdom of God first idea in Matt. 6:33.

According to Dr. Bob, the slogans Easy Does It and One day at a time came from the next verse Matthew 6:34. See Dick B., *The Good Book and The Big Book*, pp. 87-88, and other citations therein. The Big Book glowingly endorses "three little mottoes" which are "First Things First; Live and Let Live; and Easy Does It" (*Alcoholics Anonymous*, 4th ed., p. 135). Two of the three very clearly have their roots in Matthew 6:24-34.

Matthew Chapter 7

1. Taking your own inventory. Much of A.A.'s Fourth, Ninth, Tenth, and Eleventh Step actions involve looking for your own part, for your own fault in troublesome matters. This self-examination process (as part of the house-cleaning and life-changing process in the Steps) was expected to result in that which, in Appendix II of the Fourth Edition of the Big Book, became described as Athe personality change sufficient to bring about recovery from alcoholism (Big Book, p. 567). Matt. 7:3-5 states:

> And why beholdest thou the mote [speck] that is in thy brother's eye, but considerest not the beam [log] that is in thine own eye?
> Or how wilt thou say to thy brother, Let me pull the mote [speck] out of thine eye; and, behold, a beam [log] is in thine own eye.
> Thou hypocrite, first cast out the beam [log] out of thine own eye; and
> then shalt thou see clearly to cast out the mote [speck] out of thy brother's eye.

These verses from Matthew were frequently cited by A.A.'s spiritual sources as the Biblical authority for self-examination and thus finding one's own part, one's own erroneous conduct, in a relationship problem. Anne Smith specifically wrote in her spiritual journal that she must look for the "mote" in her own eye. We've already discussed similar "inventory" ideas in James.

2. Ask, seek, knock. Matt. 7:7-11 states:

> Ask, and it shall be given you; seek, and ye shall find; knock, and it shall be opened unto you;
> For every one that asketh receiveth; and he that seeketh findeth; and to him that knocketh it shall be opened.

> Or what man is there of you, whom if his son ask
> bread, will he give him a stone? Or if he ask a fish,
> will he give him a serpent?
> If ye then, being evil, know how to give good gifts
> unto your children, how much more shall your
> Father which is in heaven give good things to
> them that ask him?

Bill Wilson's spiritual teacher, Rev. Sam Shoemaker—
called by Bill a "co-founder of A.A."--wrote:

> Our part [in the crisis of self-surrender] is to
> ask, to seek, to knock. His [God's] part is to
> answer, to come, to open (Samuel M.
> Shoemaker, Jr. *Realizing Religion*. NY:
> Association Press, 1923, p. 32).

The Runner's Bible (one of the most important of the early
A.A. Bible devotionals) has an entire chapter titled, Ask
and Ye shall receive. Another favored devotional among
the A.A. pioneers was *My Utmost for His Highest*, by
Oswald Chambers. Chambers says, about the foregoing
verses beginning with Matt. 7:7:

> The illustration of prayer that Our Lord uses here
> is that of a good child asking for a good thing. . . .
> It is no use praying unless we are living as
> children of God. Then, Jesus says: Everyone that
> asketh receiveth.

The foregoing verses, and relevant comments by A.A.
sources, underline all the requisites in the asking and
receiving concept. First, you must become a child of God.
Then, establish a harmonious relationship with Him. And
only *then* expect good results from the Creator, Yahweh,
our God—expecting "Providence from Him because He is
in fact our Heavenly Father and cares about His childrens'
needs.

Given the emphasis in early A.A. on the Sermon, those verses from Matt. 7 very probably influenced similar ideas expressed as follows in the Big Book's Fourth Edition:

> If what we have learned and felt and seen means anything at all, it means that all of us, whatever our race, creed, or color are the children of a living Creator with whom we may form a relationship upon simple and understandable terms as soon as we are willing and honest enough to try (p. 28).

> God will constantly disclose more to you and to us. Ask Him in your morning meditation what you can do each day for the man who is still sick. The answers will come, *if your own house is in order.* But obviously you cannot transmit something you haven't got. See *to it that your relationship with Him is right,* and great events will come to pass for you and countless others. This is the Great Fact for us (p. 164, italics added).

In this same vein. Dr. Bob's wife, Anne, wrote, in the spiritual journal she shared with early AAs and their families:

> We can't give away what we haven't got. We must have a genuine contact with God in our present experience. Not an experience of the past, but an experience in the presentcactual, genuine (Dick B., *Anne Smith's Journal, 1933-1939. 3rd ed,* Kihei, HI: Paradise Research Publications, Inc., 1988, p. 121).

3. Do unto others. The so-called Golden Rule cannot, as such, be readily identified in A.A.'s Big Book though it certainly is a much-quoted portion of the Sermon on the Mount which Bill and Dr. Bob said underlies A.A.'s philosophy. The relevant verse is Matt. 7:12:

> Therefore all things whatsoever ye would that men should do to you, do ye even so to them: for this is the law and the prophets.

Perhaps the following two Big Book Fourth Edition segments bespeak that Golden Rule philosophy as Bill may have seen it:

> We have begun to learn tolerance, patience and good will toward all men, even our enemies, for we look on them as sick people. We have listed the people we have hurt by our conduct, and are willing to straighten out the past if we can (p. 70).

> Then you will know what it means to give of yourself that others may survive and rediscover life. You will learn the full meaning of Love thy neighbor as thyself (p. 153).

In his last address to AAs, Dr. Bob said: "Our Twelve Steps, when simmered down to the last, resolve themselves into the words 'love' and 'service.'" (*DR. BOB, supra*, pp. 77, 338).

I now know from my extensive research of the United Christian Endeavor Society, to which Dr. Bob belonged as a youngster in the North Congregational Church at St. Johnsbury, Vermont, that Christian Endeavor frequently spoke of "love and service;" and I have concluded that the original Akron fellowship's principles and practices seem very much patterned on those Dr. Bob embraced from his Christian Endeavor days. As one lead to what Dr. Bob might have taken from his early background on this point, note that Christian Endeavor's magazine was called the "Golden Rule"— which further highlights the significance of this "do unto others" concept in Dr. Bob's life and legacy. The frequent discussion by both Christian Endeavor and Dr. Bob of Biblical "love and service" can probably and appropriately be equated with the unselfish love and service implicit in the Sermon's "Golden Rule"—do unto others as you would have them do unto you.

4. He that doeth the will of my Father. There are *several* key verses in the Sermon on the Mount which could have caused Bob and Bill to say that Matthew Chapters Five to Seven contained A.A.'s underlying philosophy. The verses are in the Lords Prayer itself (Matt. 6:9-13), in the so-called Golden Rule quoted above (Matt. 7:12), and in the phrase AThy will be done (Matt. 6:10). Each or all could be considered among Dr. Bob's "fundamentals" and "essentials." In addition to these three sets of verses, however, I really believe that the major, the "fundamental," the "essential," and the "underlying" spiritual A.A. philosophy borrowed by the founders from the Sermon on the Mount can be found in Matt. 7:21:

> Not every one that saith unto me. Lord, Lord, shall enter into the kingdom of heaven; but he that doeth the will of my Father which is in heaven.

Do the will of Yahweh our Creator, Who was the Father of Jesus. That is the injunction in these last verses of the Sermon. Bill Wilson said clearly in the Big Book and in his other writings that the key requirement in A.A. is doing the will of the Father the Father Who is the *subject* of the Lord's Prayer; Almighty God –Whose will was to be done; the Creator upon whom early AAs relied as they sought to "find" and obey Him. Note that Wilson wrote:

> I was to sit quietly when in doubt, asking only for direction and strength to meet my problems as He would have me (Bill's Story, Big Book, 4th ed., p. 13).

> He humbly offered himself to his Maker then he knew (Big Book, 4th ed., p. 57).

> . . . praying only for knowledge of His will for us and the power to carry that out (Step Eleven, Big Book, 4th ed., p. 59).

> May I do Thy will always (portion of Third Step Prayer, Big Book, 4th ed., p. 63)!

> Thy will be done (Big Book, 4th ed, pp. 67, 88).

> Grant me strength, as I go out from here, to do your bidding. Amen (portion of Seventh Step Prayer, Big Book, 4th ed., p. 76).

> There is God, our Father, who very simply says, 'I am waiting for you to do my will' *(Alcoholics Anonymous Comes of Age,* p. 105).

From a long literary and religious heritage, the Oxford Group, Rev. Sam Shoemaker, and Bill Wilson acquired and expressed the simple idea that God has a plan, and that man's chief end is to accomplish that plan. See Frank Buchman, *Remaking the World*, pp. 48, 53, 63, 77, 78, 101, 144; A. J. Russell, *For Sinners Only*, p. 23; Samuel M. Shoemaker, *Children of the Second Birth*, p. 27; Dick B., *The Oxford Group and Alcoholics Anonymous*, pp. 158-160, 40-41; *New Light on Alcoholism*, p. xiii.

In his treatise, *The Ideal Life*, published in 1897, Professor Henry Drummond (also the author of *The Greatest Thing in the World*—to be discussed in a moment)—quoted the following from Acts, Chapter 23:

> And afterward they desired a king: and God gave unto them Saul. . . . And when he had removed him, he raised up unto them David to be their king: to whom also he gave testimony, and said, I have found David, the son of Jesse, a man after mine own heart, which shall fulfill all my will. Of this man's seed hath God according to his promise raised unto Israel a Saviour, Jesus (verses 21-23)

Drummond then set forth his basic theme of the "Ideal" life. It was devoted to David—"The Man After God's Own Heart: A Bible Study on the Ideal of a Christian Life." He took King David as his example because God said David was a man after His own heart—who "shall" fulfill my will. Eloquently, Drummond wrote, as part of his essays in the *The Ideal Life*:

> Now we are going to ask to-day, What is the true plan of the Christian life? We shall need a definition that we my know it, a description that we may follow it. And if you look, you will see

> that both, in a sense, lie on the surface of our text. "A man after Mine own heart,"—here is the definition of what we are to be. "Who shall fulfill all my Will."—here is the description of how we are to be it. These words are the definition and the description of the model human life. They describe the man after God's own heart. They give us the key to the Ideal Life. The general truth of these words is simply this: that the end of life is to do God's will (Henry Drummond. *The Greatest Thing in the World*. London and Glasgow: Collins Clear-Type Press, n.d., p. 203).

Dr. Bob owned all the Drummond books. I saw them as I poured over his "library" consisting of about half the books in the attic of his daughter Sue Smith Windows. I saw Drummond books in the lists Sue and her brother Smitty wrote to me in their own hand and in the books Smitty donated to Dr. Bob's Home in Akron. Dr. Bob read them. His name and address were written in his own hand in most. And Sue even phoned me shortly before her death to confirm the importance of Drummond's *Natural Law in the Spiritual World*—one of Dr. Bob's books which we had reviewed in her attic.

And what about Bill? Well, we know for sure that he at least *heard* all the Oxford Group ideas. We know he said that he and Dr. Bob felt O.G. ideas had "seeded" A.A. And Bill probably talked more about "Thy will be done" and doing God's will than any other Biblical concept he borrowed for the Big Book.

Now let's turn to a very basic question which should have been put directly to Bill Wilson and Dr. Bob: What, then, was the source of the underlying philosophy of A.A. in the Sermon?

I don't know!

Take your choice. It could have been the Lord's Prayer. It could have been "Thy will be done" in the Lord's Prayer. It could have been the Golden Rule—a probability at which Dr. Bob once hinted It could have been the Beatitudes. It could have been "love thy neighbor, and even thine enemies." It could have been "First Things First:--"seek ye first the kingdom of God and His righteousness." But the most forceful of the Sermon's declarations seemed to be:

> Not everyone that saith unto me, Lord Lord, shall enter into the kingdom of heaven; but he that doeth the will of my Father which is in heaven (Matthew 7:22).

This fundamental is also expressed in the Old Testament in these words from Ecclesiastes 12:13:

> Let us hear the conclusion of the whole matter. Fear God, and keep his commandments: for this is the whole duty of man

I like some of the following words about Bob and what Bill and others had to say about him:

> Prayer, of course, was an important part of Dr. Bob's faith. According to Paul S., "Dr. Bob's morning devotion consisted of a short prayer, a 20-minute study of a familiar verse from the Bible, and a quiet period of waiting for directions as to where he, that day, should find use for his talent. Having heard, he would religiously go about his Father's business, as he put it" (DR. BOB, supra, p. 314).

The Gospel of Luke tells us that, at age 12, Jesus "tarried behind in Jerusalem" after his parents had left.

Three days later, they found him in the temple, sitting in the midst of the doctors, both hearing them, and asking them questions. They all were astonished at his understanding and answers. His parents saw him; chewed him out for tarrying; but were than to hear Jesus reply to them:

> How is it that ye sought me? Wist ye not that I must be about my Father's business? (See Luke 2:43-49)

In other words, don't you realize that "my Father's business" comes first. Doing His will comes first. Seek ye first His kingdom. Man's whole duty is to keep His commandments.

In its biography of Dr. Bob, A.A. reported that Dr. Bob, when he was conducting surgery and wasn't sure, would pray before he started, as to which Bob commented:

> "When I operated under those conditions, I never made a move that wasn't right". . . . Whenever he got stuck about something, he always prayed about it. . . . He prayed, not only for his own understanding, but for different groups of people who requested him to pray for them, said Bill Wilson . . . "Bob was far ahead of me in that sort of activity" (*DR. BOB, supra,* pp. 314-15)

Opinions are not always held in high regard in today's A.A. But I'll have a shot at this one: I believe that endeavoring to do the will of the Creator—as it is set forth in the Bible or as God may reveal it to an individual—constitutes A.A.'s underlying philosophy as spelled out in the Sermon on the Mount, of which Bob and Bill spoke.

Part Three:

A.A.'s Connection with The Greatest Thing in the World

The Verses in 1 Corinthians 13 Were Parts of the Bible Early AAs Considered Essential

The Content of 1 Corinthians 13

1 Corinthians 13:1   Though I speak with the tongues of men and of angels, and have not charity [love], I am become [as] sounding brass, or a tinkling cymbal.

1 Corinthians 13:2   And though I have [the gift of] prophecy, and understand all mysteries, and all knowledge; and though I have all faith, so that I could remove mountains, and have not charity, I am nothing.

1 Corinthians 13:3   And though I bestow all my goods to feed [the poor], and though I give my body to be burned, and have not charity, it profiteth me nothing.

1 Corinthians 13:4   Charity suffereth long, [and] is kind; charity envieth not; charity vaunteth not itself, is not puffed up,

1 Corinthians 13:5   Doth not behave itself unseemly, seeketh not her own, is not easily provoked, thinketh no evil;

1 Corinthians 13:6   Rejoiceth not in iniquity, but rejoiceth in the truth;

105

1 Corinthians 13:7   Beareth all things, believeth all things, hopeth all things, endureth all things.

1 Corinthians 13:8   Charity never faileth: but whether [there be] prophecies, they shall fail; whether [there be] tongues, they shall cease; whether [there be] knowledge, it shall vanish away.

1 Corinthians 13:9   For we know in part, and we prophesy in part.

1 Corinthians 13:10   But when that which is perfect is come, then that which is in part shall be done away.

1 Corinthians 13:11   When I was a child, I spake as a child, I understood as a child, I thought as a child: but when I became a man, I put away childish things.

1 Corinthians 13:12   For now we see through a glass, darkly; but then face to face: now I know in part; but then shall I know even as also I am known.

1 Corinthians 13:13   And now abideth faith, hope, charity, these three; but the greatest of these [is] charity.

The Importance in A.A. of Henry Drummond's *The Greatest Thing in the World*

Long a best-seller, both before and after the founding of A.A., Professor Henry Drummond's title, *The Greatest Thing in the World*, was one of Dr. Bob's favorite books. He owned it. He studied it. He recommended it. He circulated it. And it explained in popular terms the contents of 1 Corinthians 13, which—as we have already shown—was one of the parts of the Bible that early AAs considered absolutely essential

All of Drummond's books were important to Dr. Bob.

Henry Drummond's life-span was short, beginning in August of 1851 and ending in March of 1897. But Drummond cut a deep path in Christian Evangelism and with his messages about love, the will of God, and the standards of Jesus. During 1873-1875, he "was swept into the current of the Great Mission conducted by Messrs. Moody and Sankey in Great Britain" He was recognized as having extraordinary powers of expression and appeal—drawing enthusiastic support from Dwight Moody. Though he had studied theology, Drummond had been interested in science, and he became a lecturer, and later a Professor of Natural Science in the Free Church College, in Glasgow, Scotland. His foundational book was *Natural Law in the Spiritual World* (NY: John B. Alden, 1887), and I found a copy among Dr. Bob's books.

Drummond began to impact on the student life of Edinburgh University as, year after year, he returned to give lectures on Christianity and Science and other Christian topics to students at Edinburgh University. This he did from four to six Sundays every spring. His message was carried to many universities and colleges in Europe, Africa, and Australia. Then, he delivered a series of addresses beginning with the best known of all on "The Greatest Thing in the World." The outlines of this address on Love were first heard at a Northfield Conference in the United States in 1887, though given four years earlier at a mission station service in Central Africa. For further details, *see The Greatest Thing in the World* by Henry Drummond with introduction by F. Y. Simpson. London and Glasgow: Collins Clear-Type Press, n.d. Helpful also in seeing Drummond's life as it can be related to A.A. are Mark Guldseth, *Streams*, Alaska: Fritz Creek Studios, 1982; Cuthbert Lennox, *Practical Life Work of Henry Drummond*. NY: James Pott & Co., 1901; and George Adam Smith, *Life of Henry Drummond*. NY: Hodder & Stoughton, 1901; Mel B., *Three Recovery Classics*. Lincoln, NE: iUniverse,Inc., 2004.

Drummond's best-seller was *The Greatest Thing in the World*. And it was among the books owned and circulated by Dr. Bob.

As to Drummond's impact on A.A., I'd also underscore Drummond's influence on Professor Henry B. Wright of Yale. Wright's work *The Will of God and a Man's Lifework* popularized the "Four Standards" of Jesus (See Henry B. Wright. *The Will of God and a Man's Lifework*. NY: The Young Men's Christian Association Press, 1909). It was Wright who wrote in his own hand the address he gave on "The Absolute Standards of Jesus." These had previously been articulated by Dr. Robert E. Speer in his title, *The Principles of Jesus*. NY: Fleming H. Revell, 1902. Speer's principles were called Honesty, Purity, Unselfishness, and Love. But is was Henry B. Wright who popularized Speer's "Four Standards" in Wright's *The Will of God* and called those four standards the "absolute" standards laid down by Jesus.. Thereafter, for many, Speer's "Four Standards" became Wright's "Four Absolutes"—Absolute Honesty, Absolute Purity, Absolute Unselfishness, and Absolute Love.

Professor Wright had an enormous influence on the ideas of Oxford Group founder Frank N.D. Buchman. See T. Willard Hunter, *World Changing Through Life Changing*, pp. 15-16. And Buchman was quick to appropriate and use Wright's "Four Absolutes" in his speeches, writings, and teaching. Via Oxford Group members, the Four Absolutes became well-known in early A.A..

As stated, Professor Wright had analyzed and expanded upon the biblical roots of the Four Standards of Jesus as articulated by Dr. Robert E. Speer in his title, *The Principles of Jesus, supra.* See Guldseth, *Streams, supra*, pp. 141-142.

Now what of Henry Drummond? Well, the fact is that, in fashioning his work on the Will of God, Professor Wright quoted extensively from Drummond's major work, *The Ideal Life*. London: Hodder & Stoughton, 1897. *The Ideal Life* was also among the books in Dr. Bob's library.

The upshot of all this is that Drummond, through his essay on 1 Corinthians 13, impacted directly and heavily on A.A. and its spiritual principles. We will see that in a moment as we review Dr. Bob's comments on Drummond's *The Greatest Thing in the World*.

In addition, Drummond substantially influenced the formulation of the Four Absolutes—Honesty, Purity, Unselfishness, and Love. Professor Henry B. Wright of Yale is responsible for the name "Four Absolutes" which was given to Speer's "Four Standards." But Drummond wrote much on how to know God's will; and Wright quoted Drummond's proposition that you can best learn

God's will through the cleansing process Drummond called: "Practice I Cor. 13:4-6" (Wright, *The Will of God*, *supra*, pp. 153-54, 161-62). Drummond also commented as to "practicing" 1 Corinthians 13: "If carried to its full meaning, absolute love or self-expression would also include victory over every sin" (Wright, *The Will of God*, *supra*, p. 210). Together, Drummond and Wright taught that you can know the will of God by implementing the Four Absolutes. And these "Four Absolutes" and the practice of them became touchstones for moral standards in the Oxford Group and the "yardsticks" (as Dr. Bob called them) for measuring moral behavior in A.A. itself.

The chain of influence discussed above—Speer to Drummond to Wright to Buchman to A.A.—put the Four Absolutes in the A.A. limelight. I have found that you seldom talk to an Oxford Group survivor, even today, without hearing about the Four Absolutes. Bill Wilson repeatedly indicated he was sick of hearing about them. Yet Dr. Bob claimed, for the rest of his life, that they were sound and important. Note, however, that Drummond's little book on 1 Corinthians 13 probably topped the Four Absolutes as far as nationwide popularity in A.A. is concerned. Yet it was Henry Drummond who likened "absolute love" to "practicing the nine ingredients of love" as he saw them in just a few verses of 1 Corinthians. Today, the Four Absolutes survive primarily in the memories of those AAs who held Dr. Bob in high regard. But the principles of 1 Corinthians 13 probably survive in far more depth in the little recognized and seldom explained "principles" to be practiced in A.A.'s Twelfth Step. And those principles are sprinkled throughout the Big Book even today.

Let's look at and for them in the following study of 1 Corinthians 13.

A Study of 1 Corinthians 13 in A.A.

1 Corinthians 13 is often called the Bible's love chapter because it focuses on the importance of love in action in the Christian's life. In the King James Version, the word charity is used in the verses which are speaking of love; but the underlying Greek word is *agape* which is more properly translated "love."

1. **The key ingredients of "love" as Corinthians defines them:** The most frequently quoted characteristics of love are contained in the following verses from the King James Version of the Bible (which is the version the A.A. pioneers used):

    > Charity [love] suffereth long, *and* is kind; charity envieth not; charity vaunteth not itself, is not puffed up,
    > Doth not behave itself unseemly, seeketh not her own, is not easily provoked, thinketh no evil;
    > Rejoiceth not in iniquity, but rejoiceth in the truth (1 Cor. 13:4-6).

The *New International Version*, which is much in use today, renders 1 Cor. 13:4-6:

    > Love is patient, love is kind. It does not envy, it does not boast, it is not proud.
    > It is not rude, it is not self-seeking, it is not easily angered, it keeps no record of wrongs.
    > Love does not delight in evil but rejoices with the truth.

2. Drummond's nomenclature: One of the most popular books in early A.A. was Professor Henry Drummond's study of 1 Corinthians 13. The title of his book, *The Greatest Thing in the World,* was taken from the last verse of 1 Corinthians chapter 13, which reads:

> And now abideth faith, hope, charity, these three; but the greatest of these is charity (1 Cor. 13:13).

Drummond's book was part of Dr. Bob's library, and a copy was still found in, and owned by, Dr. Bob's family when the author interviewed Dr. Bob's son and daughter several years ago. In much earlier years, A.A. Old-timer Bob E. had sent a memo to Bill Wilson's wife, Lois, in which Bob E. listed *The Greatest Thing in the World* as one of three books Dr. Bob regularly provided to alcoholics with whom he worked.

3. The unique importance to Dr. Bob of Drummond's work: Dr. Bob's enthusiasm for Drummond's book is dramatized by the following remarks of Dorothy S.M., a former wife of A.A. old-timer Clarence S. Dorothy S. M., said:

> Once, when I was working on a woman in Cleveland, I called and asked him [Dr. Bob], What do I do for somebody who is going into D.T.'s? He told me to give her the medication, and he said, When she comes out of it and she decides she wants to be a different woman, get her Drummond's >The Greatest Thing in the World.' Tell her to read it through every day for 30 days, and she'll be a different woman (See *DR. BOB and the Good Oldtimers,* p. 310).

Henry Drummond himself had made a similar suggestion half a century earlier, at the close of the lecture in which he delivered his "greatest thing in the world" addressʙthe address which was later published in Drummond's best-seller. Drummond said:

> Now I have all but finished. How many of you will join me in reading this chapter [1 Corinthians 13] once a week for the next three months? A man did that once and it changed his whole life. Will you do it? It is for the greatest thing in the world. You might begin by reading it every day, especially the verses which describe the perfect character. Love suffereth long, and is kind; loveth envieth not; love vaunteth not itself. Get these ingredients into your life (See Drummond, *The Greatest Thing in the World.* p. 53).

4. Comparing the language of Corinthians with Drummond's definitions and A.A.'s corresponding principles: The important influence on A.A. that came from 1 Corinthians 13 can be seen in Drummond's own simplified description of love's *ingredients*. Drummond listed nine ingredients of love as he saw love specifically defined in that portion of that chapter of the Bible (See Drummond, *The Greatest Thing in the World*, pp. 26-27).

And we here set out those nine love ingredients with references to correlative Bible verses and correlative A.A. language:

Drummond's Explanation	Authorized KJV	NIV Version	A.A. Big Book 4th ed. Examples
1. Patience	Charity suffereth long.	Love is patient	pp.67,70, 83, 111, 163
2. Kindness	*and* is kind.	love is kind	pp. 67, 82, 83, 86
3. Generosity	charity envieth not.	It does not envy	pp. 145, *cf.* 82
4. Humility	charity vaunteth not itself is not puffed up.	it does not boast it is not proud	pp. 13, 57, 68, 87-88
5. Courtesy	Doth not behave itself unseemly	It is not rude	p. 69
6. Unselfishness	seeketh not her own.	It is not self-seeking	pp. xxv, 93, 127
7. Good Temper	is not easily provoked	it is not easily angered	pp.19,67,70, 83-84, 125, 118
8. Guilelessness	thinketh no evil	it keeps no record of wrongs	pp. 19, 67, 70, 83-84, 118, 125
9. Sincerity	Rejoiceth not in iniquity but rejoiceth in the truth	does not delight in evil but rejoices with the truth	pp. xiv, xxvii, 13, 26, 28, 32, 44, pp. 47, 55, 57-58, 63-65, 67, 70, 73, 117, 140, 145

Love—The Love of God as the essence of the Program

1. How Drummond fits in: Dr. Bob said that A.A.'s Twelve Steps, when simmered down to the last, quite simply resolved themselves into the words love and service (See *DR. BOB and the Good Oldtimers*, p. 338). He presented God to the old-timers as a God of love who was interested in their individual lives. (*DR. BOB,* *supra*, p. 110). Dr. Bob's wife, Anne, frequently quoted the love verses in 1 John 4:8; 4:16 God is love (*DR. BOB supra*, pp. 116-17). Furthermore both Anne and her husband Dr. Bob studied Toyohiko Kagawa's book, *Love: The Law of Life.* In that book, the author Kagawa devoted an entire chapter to 1 Corinthians 13, not only to the Corinthians chapter, but also to Drummond's analysis of that chapter in Drummond's *The Greatest Thing in the World*. Hence there was much emphasis among the A.A. pioneers on the spiritual principle of love as it is defined in the Bible. In fact, the Big Book itself talks repeatedly of that principle of love (Big Book, 4th ed., pp. 83-84, 86, 118, 122, 153).

Love, then--the love of God--was a much cherished principle in early A.A. The AAs needed it, wanted it, studied it, and sought to know it. Despite the higher power aberrations in current A.A. writings and meeting talk, the love of God is still a vital component of A.A. thinking and speech. Even Bill Wilson inserted the phrase a loving God in A.A.'s Traditions. And I well remember my good A.A. friend Seymour W., a Jew, who tried each morning to comfort his many friends in the fellowship. The telephone on Seymour's God line" would ring for many about 6:00 A.M. The message to the awakened, bedraggled AA was, God loves you. And Seymour would hang up. It was a coveted privilege to be on Seymour's God-loves-you morning call list. What a way to start the day in early sobriety! And that fact of a loving God's concern for me—for each of His kids— was Seymour's message.

2. The "Great" Commandments on Love: Further illustrating the great store placed on God's love and on the Corinthians love principle by A.A. pioneers is their frequent rendition of Jesus Christ's message in Mark 12:30-31. These Gospel verses deal with what Jesus called the two *great* commandments:

> And thou shalt love the Lord thy God with all thy heart, and with all thy soul, and with all thy mind, and with all thy strength; this is the first commandment. And the second is like, namely this, Thou shalt love thy neighbor as thyself. There is none other commandment greater than these.

The foregoing verses, from the Gospel of Mark in the New Testament, were cited for the standard of ΛAbsolute Love, as it was discussed in AA of Akron's *A Manual for Alcoholics Anonymous* (one of the four pamphlets commissioned by Dr. Bob for use among early AAs). The Old Testament also contained the very same commandments to which Jesus referred, underlining the importance of love of God and of neighbor in all the commandments of the Bible. Thus, in Deuteronomy and Leviticus, the Bible says:

> Hear, O Israel: The Lord our God *is* one Lord: And thou shalt love the Lord thy God with all thine heart, and with all thy soul, and with all thy might (Deut. 6:4-5).

> Thou shalt not avenge, nor bear any grudge against the children of thy people, but thou shalt love thy neighbor as thyself: I *am* the Lord (Lev. 19:18).

A.A. literature contains no specifics on, or detailing of, the impact of, 1 Corinthians 13 on A.A. See, for example, Mel B., *Three Recovery Classics*, supra; Bill Pittman, *AA The Way It Began*. Seattle: Glen Abbey Books, 1988. But this cherished love essential, as Dr. Bob put it, deserves to be revived, promulgated, and applied today. The particulars can be seen by reading 1 Corinthians 13 itself; by noting the frequent mention of ALove in the Big Book; by studying the reading and remarks of Dr. Bob and Anne; by remembering Bill Wilson's specific mention of Corinthians; and by the repeated mention of 1 Corinthians 13 in A.A.'s religious sources.

The nine love ingredients, as they were summarized by Henry Drummond, permeate A.A.'s basic text and can fairly be proclaimed to be among those principles to be practiced at the level of A.A.'s Twelfth Step. Regrettably, Wilson just plain ignored all the principles in his Twelfth Step chapter.

The fundamental principle is, of course, love. The component ingredients or virtues involved in such love are: patience; tolerance; kindness; humility; honesty; unselfishness; consideration for others. Also the avoidance of anger, jealousy, envy, pride, and wrongdoing.

As previously made clear, almost every one of these virtues can be found in both Jesus' Sermon on the Mount and the Book of James. The principles are defined in the Sermon on the Mount in specific terms that elaborate upon what constitutes doing the will of God in the love category. And, in James, from the standpoint of action, relying on God through prayer, guidance, and obedience in service to God and service to others.

These specific aspects of love were also the very the principles of love and service of which Dr. Bob spoke in his farewell address and defined as the essence of A.A.'s spiritual program of recovery. They still represent the best in A.A.

END

Appendix 1

Outline of the Original Program

The Akron Crucible Where It All Began

(The Place Where The Cure for the "A First Forty" Was Developed Between 1935 and 1938)

The Real Program of Early A.A.

Most facets of early A.A.'s real spiritual program of recovery have received little or no attention either from present-day A.A. literature, or from historical accounts, or from A.A. groups themselves.

This account will put the full picture on record. First, it will present a brief overview of exactly what the pioneers did while they were fashioning their program in Akron between June 10, 1935 and the publication of A.A.'s Big Book in the Spring of 1939. Second, we'll see exactly how that program was summarized after an independent and objective survey by Frank Amos in 1938--a survey whose findings were embodied in reports Amos delivered to John D. Rockefeller, Jr., in response to Rockefeller's request for information about the newly discovered cure. Third, we will look briefly at what happened to the program as it wound its way to the Big Book in 1939.

An Overview of What They Did in Akron

Hospitalization for about seven days: Hospitalization and/or medical help for a brief period was virtually a "must" for most early A.A. members. During that period, only a Bible was allowed in the hospital room; medications were administered; there were daily visits and lengthy talks by Dr. Bob with the patients; there were visits by the recovered pioneer who told of their victories; there was an admission of belief in the Creator, a "surrender" to Christ, a prayer; and then release.

Recovery in the homes: Recovery work in Akron did not take place in groups or meetings or treatment centers; nor in rehabs or therapy or confinement. It took place primarily in homes, and that in itself constituted a very different situation than the one found in the Oxford Group as such. In the Akron homes, there were (1) Daily get-togethers. (2) Bible studies and reading. (3) Individual quiet times. (4) Quiet time meetings in the Smith home in the morning with Dr. Bob's wife Anne. (5) Discussions with Dr. Bob, Henrietta Seiberling, and Anne Smith. (6) A regular Wednesday meeting with "Real" surrenders upstairs after the manner of James 5:15-16 with "elders" and prayer, acceptance of Jesus Christ, asking God to take alcohol out of their lives, and asking Him to help them live by the Four Absolutes. (7) Utilization of some Oxford Group techniques such as Inventory, Confession, Conviction, and Restitution. (8) Arranging visits to newcomers at the hospital. (9) Recommended church attendance by most. (10) Recommended social, religious, and family fellowship.

The Regular Wednesday Meeting: There were no significant Oxford Group testimonials or alcoholic drunkalogs. There was a set-up meeting on Mondays where leaders sought God's guidance as to topics and leaders for the Wednesday meeting. The regular weekly meeting on Wednesday involved an opening prayer;

reading of Scripture; group prayer and seeking of guidance; discussion led by someone such as Dr. Bob, Henrietta Seiberling, or T. Henry Williams; "real" surrenders upstairs for the newcomers; arranging visits to the hospital; closing with the Lord's Prayer; socializing; and the exchange of Christian literature. No drunkalogs. No Steps. No Big Book. No texts at all. Just the Bible and devotionals like *The Upper Room.*

Quiet Times: (observed individually, by the group, and with Anne Smith). The first condition of receiving revelation is *not* listening to God. It is becoming a child of God by accepting Jesus Christ as Lord and Saviour (John 3:1-8, 16-17; 14:6; Acts 2:38, 4:12; 16:30-31; Romans 10:9; 1 Corinthians 12). Hence, the "surrender" and new birth was a vital part of the Akron program, as evidenced by the surrender at the hospital and often the real surrender in the homes. Then, for born-again believers, quiet time consisted of reading the Bible, prayer to and seeking guidance from God, use of devotionals like *The Upper Room*, utilizing Anne Smith's Journal for teaching and instruction, and reading Christian literature such as Henry Drummond's *The Greatest Thing in the World*.

The Emphasis of both Bill and Bob together: I have several times quoted or summarized the statements of Bob and Bill together on the platform of the Shrine Auditorium in Los Angeles in 1943. The remarks were reported in the March, 1943 issue of *The Tidings*. About 4500 AAs and their families were present. Bill spoke about the importance of Divine Aid, the religious element in A.A., and prayer. Dr. Bob spoke about the importance of cultivating the habit of prayer and reading the Bible. Both men were warmly received—a testimony to their harmonious accord, consistency, and simplicity of presentation when appearing together.

The Frank Amos Reports in 1938

Speaking of the alcoholics in Akron, Frank Amos reported to John D. Rockefeller, Jr.: "All considered practically incurable by physicians." Yet, said Amos, they had been reformed and so far have remained teetotalers. Their stories, he said, were remarkably alike in "the technique used and the system followed. The Amos report therefore is critically important to an understanding, verification, and validation of the commonality of what they did in Akron.

Frank Amos, who later was to become an A.A. trustee, described the seven-point Akron Program as follows:

[**Abstinence**] An alcoholic must realize that he is an alcoholic, incurable from a medical viewpoint, and that he must never again drink anything with alcohol in it.

[**Absolute reliance on the Creator**] He must surrender himself absolutely to God, realizing that in himself there is no hope.

[**Removal of sins from his life**] Not only must he want to stop drinking permanently, he must remove from his life other sins such as hatred, adultery, and others which frequently accompany alcoholism. Unless he will do this absolutely, Smith and his associates refuse to work with him.

[**Daily Quiet Time with Bible study and prayer**] He must have devotions every morning--a quiet time of prayer and some reading from the Bible and other religious literature. Unless this is faithfully followed, there is grave danger of backsliding.

[**Helping other alcoholics**] He must be willing to help other alcoholics get straightened out. This throws up a protective barrier and strengthens his own willpower and convictions.

[**Fellowship**] It is important, but not vital, that he meet frequently with other reformed alcoholics and form both a social and religious comradeship.

[**Religious affiliation**] Important, but not vital, that he attend some religious service at least once weekly.

For more on the Amos investigation and reports, see *DR. BOB and the Good Oldtimers* (NY: Alcoholics Anonymous World Services, Inc.), p. 131; Dick B., *God and Alcoholism: Our Growing Opportunity in the 21st Century* (Kihei, HI: Paradise Research Publications, Inc., 2002).

The Big Book Publication in 1939

By a very slender margin, A.A. pioneers voted in Akron to let Bill Wilson write a book about how their program worked. This he began to do in 1938 and completed in the Spring of 1939.

Plenty has been written about how the Big Book was written. However, much of the story has yet to be told, and it will not be told here. Suffice it to say that Dr. Bob said he did not write the Twelve Steps and had nothing to do with the writing of them. Though Wilson submitted drafts of the Big Book to Dr. Bob, very few in Akron reviewed them; and practically no changes were proposed by the Akron pioneers. Wilson, however, made very substantial changes which inserted Power and higher power and some new thought verbiage such as Czar of the Universe. He added New Thought or "New Age" expressions like fourth dimension. He eliminated all specific references to the Bible, all specific reference to fundamental Oxford Group ideas such as the Four Absolutes, the Five C's, and Jesus Christ. He made reference to supposed six word-of-mouth steps that he said were used in the formative years. But he described them in many different ways at varying times. Comments about a flying blind period began to be hurled at Akron's work. And ultimately, Wilson fashioned Twelve Steps which he said *were* the Steps the A.A. newcomers *had taken* to find God, establish a relationship with Him, and have a spiritual experience that would give them a daily reprieve from their alcoholism.

Most of us in A.A. today believe we are "taking" steps that were taken by early A.A. people. But, of course, *we are not*. And we may eventually come to realize that fact.

How do we know that the idea that steps were "taken" is a complete fabrication? First, Bill had been commissioned to write a book about how the *Akron experiment had worked.* He did not. For that matter, there were no steps at all in the Akron program. Second, there were no Steps in any program when Bill wrote his Big Book. The Oxford Group had no Steps whatever. It did not have four steps (as one writer contends), not six (as Bill sometimes contended), and certainly not Twelve. Nor did A.A. have any Steps. Dr. Bob said so, and that's good enough for me. Further, you'll find no mention of steps in the stories that accompanied the First Edition that was published in 1939.

Bill simply fashioned his own text, his own program, and his own steps. He utilized the Oxford Group principles for the heart of his own program of recovery. And he added chapters for agnostics, wives, employers, families, and so on.

All Bill's earlier references to cure, to reformed alcoholics, and to ex drunkards were discarded. Special attention was given to agnostics with a formula for them to choose their own conception of God. These material alterations by Wilson presented an entirely new program.

It goes without saying that the Wilson text book was totally different from the simple program pursued in Akron, described by Frank Amos, and productive of the 75% rate. What Wilson did do was to incorporate into his Big Book most of the words, phrases, and practices of the Oxford Group and Sam Shoemaker though there is little acknowledgment of this fact in the Big Book. For the striking resemblances of Big Book language to the language of Shoemaker and the Oxford Group writings, see Dick B., *New Light on Alcoholism*, *The Oxford Group and Alcoholics Anonymous*, *Turning Point*, *Twelve Steps for You*, *Anne Smith's Journal*, and *By the Power of God*.

END

Appendix 2

Comparing the Christian Endeavor Root

Preliminary Glimpses at Christian Endeavor from Its Founding through the days of Dr. Bob's Participation

The Genesis of the Christian Endeavor Society

The first Christian Endeavor society was organized on February 2, 1881. See Francis E. Clark. *Christian Endeavor in all Lands*. Boston, MA: The United Society of Christian Endeavor, 1886, pp. 35, 41, 621.

Rev. Francis E. Clark, pastor of Williston Church in Portland, Maine, formed the society in the parlor of his home at 62 Neal Street—the parsonage of Williston Church. Members consisted of boys and girls in the "Mizpah Circle"—a missionary circle for young people which was led by the pastor's wife. During the February Mizpah meeting, Clark framed a constitution for the society and called it "Williston Young People's Society of Christian Endeavor." He wrote that the "greatest stress was on the *religious* features;" the society was to be "an out-and-out Christian society;" and the activities "were to centre around the weekly young people's prayer meeting."

W. H. Pennell, the teacher of the Young Men's Bible Class, then carefully explained to the circle members the society and its constitution, and led all the young people present in signing the new constitution. Several clauses of the constitution are historically instructive and bear repeating here. For the further details on the foregoing and following points and the constitution itself, see Francis E. Clark. *Memories of Many Men in Many Lands: An Autobiography*. Boston, MA: United Society of Christian Endeavor, 1922. Clark wrote at pp. 77-87:

> "Object. Its object shall be to promote an earnest Christian life among its members, to increase their mutual acquaintance, and to make them more useful in the service of God. . . .
>
> "Officers. The officers of this society shall be a President, Vice President and   Secretary. There shall also be a Prayer meeting Committee of five a Social Committee of five, and a Lookout Committee of Five.
>
> "Duties of Officers. . . . The Prayer meeting Committee shall have in charge the Friday evening prayer-meeting;
>
> "The Prayer-meeting. It is expected that all the members of the society will be present at every meeting unless detained by some absolute necessity and that each one will take some part however slight in every meeting. The meetings will be held just one hour and at the close some time may be taken for introductions and social intercourse if desired. Once each month an Experience meeting shall. . . [Note that the remaining portions of this sentence were not shown in Clark's autobiography]."

A Brief Digression: The Period of Dr. Bob's Youth.

Perhaps not by accident, A.A.'s own "Conference Approved" literature has chosen to report little about

Dr. Bob's youth. This gaping hole might, I believe, explain many of the omissions in the traditional A.A. Timeline stories. On the other hand, the absence of facts may be a blessing for those of us who are taking a fresh start, a fresh approach, and a fresh viewpoint when it comes to the history of early A.A.

The initial question here concerns just exactly what Dr. Bob did as a youngster in the North Congregational Church at St. Johnsbury, Vermont, and just exactly what he was seeing, hearing, learning, and practicing in the Christian Endeavor Society at his church and even elsewhere. Those questions are being researched in much depth right now!

Meager though the details are, here's what A.A. itself does tell us about Dr. Bob's youth. And these facts can, in turn, provide an adequate start and framework pointing us toward many more details as to his early religious years and religious training.

Robert Holbrook Smith was born August 8, 1879 in the family home at Central and Summer Streets in St. Johnsbury, Vermont. Judge and Mrs. Walter Perrin Smith were his parents. The Judge had a distinguished career as Probate Judge, state's attorney, state legislator, superintendent of St. Johnsbury schools, director of one bank, and president of another. He died in 1918; and he had taught Sunday school for 40 years! Dr. Bob's mother was said to have felt "that the way to success and salvation lay through strict parental supervision, no-nonsense education, and regular spiritual devotion."

From 1885 to 1894, Bob went to Summer Street Elementary School, two blocks from his home. In 1894, Bob was 15 years old and entered St. Johnsbury Academy—an independent secondary school "for the intellectual, moral, and religious training of boys and girls in northeastern Vermont." In his senior year at St. Johnsbury, he met Anne Ripley, his bride-to-be, at a dance in the academy gym. Seventeen years later, they were married. Bob graduated from St. Johnsbury Academy in 1898. He then set off for four years at Dartmouth College, sixty miles south at Hanover, New Hampshire. He graduated in 1902 and by that time was an illustrious graduate of the college drinking "fraternity."

Sadly—in contrast to the endless biographies, stories of, by, and about, Bill Wilson and his life—A.A. has devoted only 23 pages to the foregoing general facts in its official biography of Bob's life (See *DR. BOB and the Good Oldtimers: A Biography, with recollections of early A.A. in the Midwest.* NY: Alcoholics Anonymous World Services, Inc., 1980, pp. 1-23). Regrettably, most of these A.A. pages contain little more of religious and spiritual significance—mostly just a Dr. Bob drunkalog, and this not even in the words of Dr. Bob.

As to Bill Wilson, Bill himself, A.A., and a host of biographers have provided us with trivial, unending, minutia about Wilson's birth behind a bar, his renunciation of church, his atheism, his grandfather, his mother, his father, his sister, his boomerang, his violin, his first love, his second love and wife-to-be Lois, his Burr and Burton Academy days, a hobo motorcycle ride, his stock market meanderings, Lois's Swedenborgian religion, the involvement of Lois's family in

Swedenborgianism, and the pair's marriage in the Swedenborgian church, as well as some information about Bill's Army days and law school attendance.

As to Dr. Bob, we AAs have been favored with very little. There is nothing about Judge Smith's religious convictions, activities, and teachings to Bob. There is nothing about Grandma Smith's religious beliefs, activities, and communications with her son on those matters. There is nothing about the family's membership in St. Johnsbury's North Congregational Church. There is nothing about that church's prayer meetings, church services, Bible studies, and quiet hours. There is nothing about the nature of its Christian Endeavor Society; and there is nothing about the Christian Endeavor activities of that particular church society or about the logs that were kept of its members and of the content of its meetings. Nor is there any mention of what Bob learned in the religious realm as a youth from the church, from the Bible, from Christian Endeavor, from his parents, or from the religious ideas taught at the academy he attended. And that is where part of our research is now directed. You as readers are invited to dig in with the same diligence A.A.'s have devoted to Rowland Hazard's drinking habits, Ebby Thacher's later years, Bill's royalty battles, Bill's girl friends, and so on. What we present here is just a launching pad for the journey into those principles and practices from Dr. Bob's youth which really shaped the early program, practices, and cures in Akron A.A.

Christian Endeavor Growth From 1881 to 1902— the date of Dr. Bob's graduation from college at Dartmouth.

The growth of Christian Endeavor from its twenty member society in Williston Church in 1881 to its status at the time of Dr. Bob's graduation from college in 1902 is absolutely astonishing. Though Congregational in origin, Christian Endeavor met the needs of youth and the need of churches of various Protestant denominations to court, encourage, and instruct young people in the service of Christ. Its influence on churches and youngsters became world-wide in span and duration.

By the time its founder Dr. Francis Clark had written his autobiography in 1922, Christian Endeavor could say that eighty thousand organizations bore its name (Clark, *Memoirs*, *supra*, p. 699). It could and did say that three hundred thousand people attended one hundred and fifty different sessions at its 1899 Convention in Detroit (Clark, *Christian Endeavor*, *supra*, p. 368). It could and did estimate that about 250,000 Endeavorers every year were joining the evangelical churches of the world (Clark, *Christian Endeavor*, *supra*, p. 338). An online encyclopedia archive on Francis Clark recorded that, in 1908, United Christian Endeavor had 70,761 societies and more than 3,500,000 members scattered throughout the United States, Canada, Great Britain, Australia, South Africa, India, Japan and China.

Let's compare the foregoing outreach of Christian Endeavor at the time of Dr. Bob's youth, as to its historical significance, with Wilson's much-discussed Washingtonian Society—a movement in the century before A.A.'s founding. The Washingtonian Society membership, said Wilson, "passed the hundred thousand mark," but, said he, it lost sight of its goal of helping alcoholics. It became embroiled in Abolition and Temperance matters, quickly faded from the scene after only a few short years of activity, and had been long dead for a good many decades before A.A. was founded (See Wilson's remarks quoted in *Pass It On*. NY: Alcoholics Anonymous World Services, Inc., 1984, pp. 325, 354, 366-367; and *Twelve Steps And Twelve Traditions*. NY: Alcoholics Anonymous World Services, Inc., 1952, pp. 178-179). Furthermore, several perspicacious AAs were later to write that **the real failure of the Washingtonian movement was its non-reliance on God and its focus on temperance pledges. And neither of these diminishing factors had anything to do with A.A.'s original form or subsequent growth!**

Let's also look at the "Oxford Group"—the much discussed yet maligned "root" of Bill Wilson's enduring Twelve Steps. At the time of its beginnings, in 1922, its members simply consisted of a small group of Rev. Frank Buchman's traveling friends who had formed what they called "A First Century Christian Fellowship" which soon faded away as a group. See Garth Lean. *Frank Buchman: A Life*. London: Constable, 1985, p. 97.

Now, let's present and compare a timeline of Christian Endeavor from its founding in 1881 to the time of Dr. Bob's graduation from Dartmouth in 1902. As we do, you can readily see its growth, tremendous size, outreach, and endurance as a real world-wide Christian fellowship that far surpassed anything else of that nature in the pre-AA history scene. From humble beginnings just before Dr. Bob's youth, this Christian movement had grown to behemoth size and worldwide membership by the time of Dr. Bob's maturity. Here is the timeline:

1879 – Dr. Bob was born in St. Johnsbury, Vermont.

1881 - February 2, the first society was organized in Williston Church, Maine.

1881 - October 8, the second society organized in the North Church, Newburyport, Mass.

Before 1882 dawned, there were at least three or four other societies—one in a Christian church in Rhode Island; another in the St. Lawrence Church of Portland; another in Burlington, Vermont.

1882 – June 2 – the first convention was held in Williston Church with six societies of less than 500 members represented and others known to exist.

1883 – 1891 – Societies were rapidly formed in Canada, Hawaii, Ceylon, Foochow, Africa, England, Australia, Turkey, Japan, Spain, France, Samoa, Mexico, and Chile. With large conventions in those years and many societies.

1892 – Eleventh Annual Convention was held at Madison Square Garden. Attendance: 30,000.

1893 – 1896 – Societies and conventions involved China, Japan, the Army, South Africa, Switzerland, Germany, Laos, Scotland, Marshall Islands, India, Hawaii, Guatemala, the Caroline Islands, Italy, Bulgaria, Mexico, and Burma.

1897 – Sixteenth International Convention in San Francisco. 25,000 journeyed across the continental United States to be a part of the outreach and activity.

1898 – 1902 – Societies and conventions were organized and met in India, Russia, Philippines, Jamaica, Portugal, and Persia.

By contrast, the Washingtonians were washed up in only a few years. And long before Dr. Bob was born or A.A. was a twinkle in Bill Wilson's eye. The Oxford Group finally did gain world-wide notice in the 1930's— only to face stiff opposition from the Roman Catholic hierarchy; run afoul of thorny claims of Buchman's supposed Nazi affiliations; become wrongfully associated with the anti-war views of some at Oxford [not, however, connected with Buchman's people]; and repeatedly have to deal with Frank Buchman's sexual investigations of earlier years. Unlike the Washingtonians, Christian Endeavor, or A.A., the Oxford Group itself was basically a one-man charisma show; and it soon found itself splitting in several directions a decade after World War II. Its survival today is in a markedly different form from that of Frank Buchman's A First Century Christian Fellowship of the 1920's and 1930's.

Yet, in the twenty years beginning with 1891, Christian Endeavor had stayed afloat, grown, gained support in many denominations, spawned similar societies in others, and acquired tens of thousands of identifiable adherents. It had literature, books, periodicals, newspapers, conventions, world conferences, offices, officers and trustees, hymnals, summer schools, training schools, and an ever-increasing support and growth rate. In sum, there was absolutely nothing like Christian Endeavor that was similar in form, content, significance, and size during the years prior to or at the time A.A.s conception or actual formative years— nothing at all like the Christian Endeavor Society which was to help instruct and train Dr. Bob in his youth, and which emphasized Bible, Church, Prayer Meetings, Quiet Hours, God, Jesus Christ, fellowship, service and witness (For details, see Clark, *Christian Endeavor, supra*, pp. 34-88, 621-628).

It is no surprise to me, however, that (given today's secularized recovery treatment approaches) the world-wide Christian Endeavor picture has remained in the dark—completely unnoticed in today's "any god" and "not-god" treatment world. The theme today seems to be: If you want to talk about Jesus, the Bible, and A.A.'s Christian roots, do it somewhere besides A.A., a treatment center, or university, a medical article, or a government periodical.

The Christian Endeavor Society Pledge, Principles, and Practices

The Christian Endeavor Covenant and Pledge
The active member's pledge used in most societies is as follows:

> "Trusting in the Lord Jesus Christ for strength, I promise Him that I will strive to do whatever He would like to have me do; that I will make it a rule of my life to pray and to read the Bible every day, and to support my own church in every way, especially by attending all her regular Sunday and midweek services, unless prevented by some reason which I can

conscientiously give to my Saviour; and that, just so far as I know how, throughout my whole life, I will endeavor to lead a Christian life. As an active member I promise to be true to all my duties, to be present at and take some part, aside from singing, in every Christian Endeavor prayer-meeting, unless hindered by some reason which I can conscientiously give to my Lord and Master. If obliged to be absent from the monthly consecration meeting of the society, I will, if possible, send at least a verse of Scripture to be read in response to my name at roll-call" (Clark, *Christian Endeavor*, *supra*, pp. 251-252).

Interesting also are the first two of six covenants in the prison-societies of Christian Endeavor:

"First. I will accept Jesus as my Lord and Saviour.

"Second. I will try to learn and do His will by forming the habit of praying and carefully reading my Bible daily, and by thinking, speaking, and acting as I believe He would in my place. . . ." (Clark, *Christian Endeavor*, *supra*, p. 253).

The founder, Rev. Clark, said the Christian Endeavor covenant has thus been analyzed:

"First, I will read the Bible.
"Second, I will pray.
"Third, I will support my own church.
"Fourth, I will attend the weekly prayer-meeting of the society.
"Fifth, I will take some part in it, aside from singing.

"Sixth, I will perform a special duty at the consecration-meeting if obliged to be absent" (Clark, *Christian Endeavor, supra,* pp 244-45).

Amos R. Wells, a prolific Endeavor writer, editor, and leader, wrote the following quips n his book *The Endeavorer's Daily Companion:*

"Don't believe in daily prayer and Bible-reading?
"Don't believe in taking part in prayer-meetings?
"Don't believe in going to church?
"Don't believe in supporting your own church?
"Don't believe in doing Christ's will?
"Don't believe in leading a Christian life?
"Don't believe in *trying* to do all these things?
"Don't believe in *promising* to try to do them?
"Why, of course you do when it is put that way! This is all you promise in the pledge—just to try to do them; and the pledge expressly says that you are not to do them whenever you think Christ would excuse you from them. Certainly no less excuse should satisfy you, pledge or no pledge" (Clark, *Christian Endeavor, supra,* p. 245).

Though we are getting ahead of ourselves in this appendix and as to later proposed research, we believe any real student of Dr. Bob's remarks will find that this A.A. co-founder was still doing the daily prayer and Bible-reading, was still conducting prayer-meetings, was still going to church, was still supporting his church, was still talking about doing his Master's will, was still emphasizing the leading of a Christian life, and was not only talking about these things throughout his A.A. years, but was urging these things on his "pigeons"—as he called the new AAs.

Assuredly, I have found no significant talk in Christian Endeavor about the Four Absolutes of the Oxford Group; nor about a life-changing "art" of self-examination, confession of sins to another person, conviction, or a "conversion" leading to a spiritual awakening. Nor even about some of pioneer A.A.'s own favored ideas in the Book of James, including James 5:16. From this I can confidently say that I have found little or nothing in Christian Endeavor history that resembled the recovery program Bill Wilson fashioned in his Twelve Steps.

The Christian Endeavor Pledge really describes the simple early A.A. Akron program in bright colors. And, if you add to the CE program, A.A.'s insistence on abstinence and hospitalization for real alcoholics, and toss in some other Christian Endeavor principles and practices, you have the very program that Dr. Bob, his wife Anne, Henrietta Seiberling, and the Williams couple were holding forth for the deliverance of those early drunks. Let's be clear, however, that my remarks do not ignore or discount the important Oxford Group backdrop and ideas that came to Akron from 1931 forward and their influence on the little Akron A.A. fellowship.

The Christian Endeavor Principles

Rev. Clark believed that the following four principles are the "roots of the Christian Endeavor tree." They are, he wrote, the essential and only essential principles of the Christian Endeavor Society:

1. Confession of Christ.
2. Service for Christ.

3. Fellowship with Christ's people.
4. Loyalty to Christ's Church.

As to each of the four, Clark said the following, among other things:

"[Confession of Christ] *Confession of Christ* is absolutely necessary in the Christian Endeavor Society. To ensure this are the methods of the Society adapted in every particular. . . . The true Christian Endeavorer does not take part to exhibit his rhetoric, or to gain practice in public speaking, or to show what a logical prayer he can offer to God; but he does take part to show that he is a Christian, to confess his love for his Lord; and this confession is as acceptable made by the unlearned, stumbling, lisping Christian as by the glib and ready phrase-maker. . . The covenant pledge is simply a tried and proved device to secure frequent confession of Christ. . . . Our form of confession is the prayer-meeting. Here we acknowledge our faith.

"[Service] Another universal principle of Christian Endeavor is *constant service*. If confession is the lungs of the movement, service is its hands and feet. . . . In the ideal society every member is responsible for some definite, particular task. . . . a society whose ideal, like Wesley's is, 'At it, and all at it, and always at it.'

"[Fellowship] Again, I have learned that *our fellowship* is an essential feature of Christian Endeavor. . . . This fellowship is not an accident or a matter of chance. It is an inevitable result of the movement. When the second society was formed, nineteen years ago, the fellowship began. Then it became interdenominational, interstate, international, intersocial, intercontinental, and, as some one has suggested, since 'Part of the hosts have crossed the flood, And part are crossing now,' it has become intermundane.

"[Loyalty manifested by love for Christ and service to church] Once more, a universal essential of the Society of Christian Endeavor is *fidelity* to its own church and the work of that church. It does not and cannot exist for itself . . . a true society of Christian Endeavor must live for Christ and the church. Its confession of love is for Christ, the head, its service is for the church, His bride. . . ."

Clark concludes with this commentary on the fundamental, necessary features of the world-wide movement:

"Confession of our love for Christ—devoting ourselves to our Lord and Saviour, Jesus Christ, so that we do not simply rely on His work of propitiation, finished on the cross, but view Him as our living King, whose will is law in every department of life.

"Proof of it by our service for Him—receiving constant religious training for all kinds of service involved in the various committees.

"Fellowship with those who love Him—interdenominational spiritual fellowship, through which we hope not for organic unity, but to realize our Lord's prayer for spiritual unity, that all who believe in Him may be one.

"Fidelity to our regiment in which we fight for
Him—strenuous loyalty to the local church and
denomination with which each society is
connected."

For more on the Christian Endeavor principles, see
Clark, *Christian Endeavor*, *supra*, pp. 89-102. And we
will say more shortly about the importance of "love and
service," in both Christian Endeavor and in Dr. Bob's
view of Alcoholics Anonymous. In fact, Dr. Bob's love
and service principles fairly leap at you from their
Christian Endeavor roots.

The Bible – As Sourcebook, Subject of Study, and as to Quotation of Verses

In early A.A., the Bible was the primary and essential
source of the basic recovery program ideas. AAs read
and were told to read it daily. Circulated literature
centered on the Bible. Bible *study* was stressed, and the
Bible was read at the beginning of each meeting. When
asked about a program question, Dr. Bob would usually
say: "What does it say in the Good Book?" He also
frequently quoted relevant verses to AAs and their
families as A.A.'s *DR BOB* does report. Until very
recently when I was in Akron on research, Dr. Bob's
Bible (with inscriptions by him, Bill Wilson, and Bill
Dotson—AA Number Three) was still brought to the
front of the A.A. Number One (King School Group)
meeting room and there remained until the meeting
was over. Each early AA meeting had a topic, and the
topic was usually based on some Bible idea, segment,
or application (See Dick B., *The Good Book and The Big
Book*; *The Akron Genesis of Alcoholics Anonymous*;
Why Early A.A. Succeeded; and *When Early AAs Were
Cured and Why*).

The Bible occupied no less prominent a place in Christian Endeavor.

The earliest Christian Endeavor journal was called *The Golden Rule* with Rev. Clark as its editor-in chief (Clark, *Christian Endeavor, supra,* pp. 82, 622; *Memories, supra,* pp. 92, 97-98). See also Matthew 7:12 for one rendition of that "golden rule" language.

The covenant pledge was, along with several other stated purposes, designed to secure "familiarity with the Word of God by promoting Bible-reading and study in preparation for every meeting" (Clark, *Christian Endeavor, supra,* p. 94). As mentioned, the first point in the analysis of the covenant is "I will read the Bible." The pledge itself says: "that I will make it the rule of my life to pray and to read the Bible every day. . ." "Every Endeavor meeting has its topic, with many Scripture references and abundant helps." "The Golden Rule . . . offered as a premium at one time the well-known 'International Bible,' a famous teacher's Bible with notes by eminent scholars." (Clark, *Christian Endeavor, supra,* pp. 244, 252, 261, 293).

Bible study was often the subject of oratory at Christian Endeavor Conventions. Speaking on some Christian Endeavor Principles, Rev. Russell H. Conwell—a favorite convention speaker—said: "I believe that a pledge is a good thing. . . . Hence I believe in the Christian Endeavor pledge to speak every week in the meeting; it makes men. I believe in the advice of studying the Holy Bible for itself; it makes men" (Clark, *Christian Endeavor, supra,* p. 606). Said to be the greatest preacher in England of his time, the Rev. Dr. J. H. Jowett said at the British National Convention in

Glasgow: "Let your endeavor grow out of the great and studious contemplation of the great mysteries in Christ" and Jowett was speaking on "Christian Endeavor and Bible-Study" (Clark, *Christian Endeavor*, *supra*, pp. 608-609).

Writing on the non-denominational and international character of Christian Endeavor, Count Bernstorff, an eminent German Christian, wrote: "There is only one Christianity, because there is only one Christ. Is it English that one insists upon conversion. . . . Is it English to avow a oneness of spirit with Christians of other denominations. . . . Is it English that one should seek after holiness. . . . Is it English that all Christians should work together for the upbuilding of Christ's kingdom? All these things are simple biblical truths, and should be the universal spirit of Christendom. Indeed, they constitute living Christendom" (Clark, *Christian Endeavor*, *supra*, pp. 618-619).

There is s vast amount of information about the Bible in the Christian Endeavorer's life and meetings; and some of it will be discussed here. Most of it is being sought and researched right now. I leave you with this recent finding by A. A. Historian Richard K, contained in the foreword to Rev. Francis E. Clark's *World Wide Endeavor*:

> "The Pledge requires daily reading of the Bible and prayer. This covenant kept makes spiritually-minded young people" [Rev. B.B. Tyler, D.D., Pastor, First Church of Disciples of Christ, New York City] (Clark, *World Wide Endeavor*, p. 7).

Richard K. also located the following remarks by J. F. Cowan in his title, *New Life in the Old Prayer Meeting.* In his chapter entitled "More Bible and Less Topic." Cowan wrote:

"Shakespeare, and Drummond, and Spurgeon, and Milton, and Meyer, and Moody, and other good men may be quoted profitably in a prayer-meeting as sidelights on the Word of God, but never to the exclusion of the Word of God. God's Word is a lamp; they are only reflectors. A hundred of the brightest reflectors are no substitute for a lamp. Literary quotations are not out of place in a prayer-meeting; but let us light the lamp before we hang up the reflectors.

"A prayer-meeting with too much topic and not enough Bible is like a farm on which some one should try to substitute moonlight for sunlight. Moonlight is good for skating, and drives, and walks, but for raising corn and wheat, and for all the vital processes of life moonlight would be a poor substitute for sunlight. Let us have the sunlight first in our prayer-meetings, and after we have got God's thought then it is time enough to have men's thoughts on God's thoughts. This is an age in which we are using too much peptonized [pre-digested] spiritual food: too many of us are getting our knowledge of the Bible at second hand, through books or daily devotions, through Sunday-school lessons, and the 'meditations' of others in published form. We need to get more of the Bible at first hand, and less of men's thoughts on God's thoughts, meditating ourselves, and being devout without a model. There is too much of the canning factory in our modern religious life, and not enough of the garden and farm."

Perhaps many have wondered why Dr. Bob's wife Anne wrote in, and widely shared from, her journal, that the Bible should be the main sourcebook of all. Also why AA meetings started first with the reading of the Bible. Also, why Dr. Bob and those who followed conventional meditation guidelines began their quiet time first with the Bible. Such also was the suggested practice in the devotional books the pioneers studied and used, and which laid out guides for quiet time.

The Christian Endeavor Prayer-Meetings – their content and importance

The discussion above deals with the primacy of the Bible and also J. F. Cowan's remarks about that. Then too, in his chapter entitled "More Prayer in the Prayer Meeting," Cowan held forth equally simple principles as to prayer. He wrote:

> "To be sure, no prayer-meeting leader should object to a personal testimony, or to any contribution calculated to edify, but at the same time there is great need in the average prayer meeting, of developing the volume of prayer. How may this be done?
>
> 1. By helping the people to understand what prayer is. There may be a great deal of prayer in the meeting that does not go by the name of prayer. There may be much that goes by the name of prayer that is not broad, symmetrical, Scriptural prayer. It may be helpful, here, to analyze prayer into some of its constituent elements; for example, as Mr. Moody did: (1) Adoration. . . (2) Confession. . . (3) Restitution. . . (4) Thanksgiving. . . (5) Forgiveness. . . (6) Unity. . . (7) Faith. . . (8) Petition. . . (9) Submission. The "Thy will be done" spirit that characterizes true prayer."

Dr. Bob's wife Anne reviewed a similar group of specific prayer definitions in *Anne Smith's Journal,* and she shared them with AAs and their families. Moreover, many years after A.A.'s founding, Rev. Sam Shoemaker was speaking to AAs at their International Convention. He defined a "spiritual awakening" as having four elements—conversion, prayer, fellowship, and witness. He also was quick to point out that "absurd names for God" and "half-baked prayers" were not a legitimate part of the awakening. Consider too that Akron AAs were exposed to much more about prayer than "half-baked" prayers. As I pointed out in *Dr. Bob and His Library*, Dr. Bob read and circulated a large number of books on prayer, quiet time, and how to pray.

Dr. Amos R. Wells was Editorial Secretary of the United Society of Christian Endeavor. His text-book on meetings and methods tell us much about the prayer meetings. He wrote:

> *"What are the results we may gain from the prayer meeting*? They are five: original thought on religious subjects; open committal to the cause of Christ; the helpful expression of Christian thought and experience; the cultivation of the spirit of worship through public prayer and through singing; the guidance of others along these lines of service and life.

> *"How can we get original thought on the prayer-meeting topics*? Only by study of the Bible, followed by meditation and observation. First, the Endeavorer should read the Bible passage; then he should read some good commentary upon it; then he should take the subject with him into his daily life for five or six days, thinking about it in his odd minutes and

watching for experiences in his own life, or the lives of others, or of observing nature and looking for illustrations on the subject from all these sources.

"Are we to read Bible verses and other quotations? Yes, all we please, if we will make them the original expression of our own lives by thinking about them, and adding to them something, if only a sentence, to show that we have made them our own. Always give the writer's name, or the part of the Bible from which you quote. Commit the quotation to memory and do not read it" (Amos R. Wells, *Expert Endeavor: A Text-book of Christian Endeavor Methods and Principle*s. Boston: United Society of Christian Endeavor, 1911, pp. 9-11; Dick B., *Dr. Bob and His Library*, p. 114; *The Books Early AAs Read for Spiritual Growth*, 7th ed., pp. 13-17).

A recent find by Richard K. covers several Christian Endeavor subjects. Bible study is certainly one. So is prayer; and Richard found that the famous evangelist and Christian Endeavor influence Dwight L. Moody wrote on the importance of prayer meetings in his title *Golden Counsels* in the chapter, "How to Have a Good Prayer Meeting' (D. L. Moody. *Golden Counsels.* Boston: United Society of Christian Endeavor, 1899, pp. 27-33).

We now know that Dr. Bob's wife taught early AAs and their families that the Bible should be the main source book of all and that not a day should pass without reading it. We know that Dr. Bob did read it every day. We know that it was read at every one of the pioneer meetings and each morning at the quiet times conducted by Anne Smith at the Smith home. And we know how often Dr. Bob quoted Scripture to make some point to AAs. At the early A.A. meetings, Bible "topics" were common, and many topics resembled those suggested by and used in Christian Endeavor prayer-meetings. To be sure, there were some limited "testimonies." But Dr. Bob specifically commented that their (the early AAs') "stories" didn't amount to much. However, there certainly was group prayer in the pioneer Christian Fellowship meetings. Actually, those meetings were, in effect, "old fashioned prayer meetings."—the essence of the Christian Endeavor program (See *DR. BOB and the Good Oldtimers, supra,* pp. 56, 71-72, 96-97, 100-102, 111, 116, 118-119, 129-136, 139-142, 144, 150-151; Dick B., *Anne Smith's Journal, 1933-1939*). Dr. Bob's son commented to me that the meetings were like "old fashioned revival meetings." Another pioneer, quoted in A.A. literature, called them "old fashioned prayer meetings."

And that's a fairly useful label to be used in contrasting Christian Endeavor prayer-meetings with the kind of "Oxford Group" meetings and house-parties that Bill and Lois continuously attended on the East Coast from the beginning of Bill's sobriety in 1934. The emphasis in the Oxford Group meetings Bill attended in the East was certainly not on prayer-meetings. It was on *testimonies* about how lives had been changed through Oxford Group techniques. Their "sharing for witness" "attested" that God had done for them what they could not do for themselves. In Akron, however, the emphasis in their Christian Fellowship meetings was on Bible reading, group prayer, topics, and upstairs "surrenders" to Christ by newcomers. In sum, Akron AA meetings focused on Bible and prayer in "old fashioned prayer" or "old fashioned revival meetings" while Oxford Group

meetings elsewhere emphasized life-changing in those
meetings and testimonies confirming change. The
difference between East Coast Oxford Group activity
and the "clandestine lodge" of the Oxford Group in
Akron becomes even more clear when you look at what
Bill said to T. Henry and Clarace Williams when Bill was
interviewing the pair in 1954. Bill said to Mr. and Mrs.
Williams:

> "I learned a great deal from you people [Mr. and
> Mrs. Williams], from the Smiths themselves, and
> from Henrietta [Seiberling]. I hadn't looked in the
> Bible, up to this time at all" (From the transcript of
> Bill Wilson's taped interview with T. Henry and
> Clarace Williams on December 12, 1954, which
> transcript is on file at General Services in New
> York. See also Dick B., *The Akron Genesis of
> Alcoholics Anonymous*, pp. 136-137).

The Quiet Hour – A Regular Endeavor Observance and a Required AA Pioneer Practice

"Quiet Time" was a "must" in early Akron A.A.; and, as
trustee-to-be Frank Amos reported it, "He [the alcoholic]
must have devotions every morning—a 'quiet time of
prayer and some reading from the Bible and other
religious literature." Amos added: "The A.A. members of
that time did not consider meetings necessary to maintain
sobriety. They were simply 'desirable.' Morning devotion
and 'quiet time,' however, were musts" (*DR. BOB, supra*,
pp. 131, 136).

At another point, Bill Wilson added: "I sort of always felt
that something was lost from A.A. when we stopped
emphasizing the morning meditation." (See *DR. BOB,
supra*, p. 178).

Unfortunately, almost all A.A. writers and AA history writers have mischaracterized A.A. quiet times. Possibly because they were steering wide and clear of Jesus Christ and the Bible. Probably because they did not mention and did not want to mention the prerequisite "born again" surrenders. Mostly because they did not do their homework.

In the first place, A.A. quiet time was and could be an individual thing, a morning thing, or a group thing; and it often was all of these. Secondly, some of the Oxford Group quiet time trappings of "journaling," "listening," writing down thoughts, and "checking" were just not a significant, if even relevant, part of Akron pioneer quiet times. Finally, almost invariably, A.A. revisionist-writers have left out the absolute necessity posited in Akron that one must first become a child of God in order to pray effectively to, and hear from, God, their "Heavenly Father." See Dick B., *Good Morning: Quiet Time, Morning Watch, Meditation, and Early A.A.*; *The Oxford Group and Alcoholics Anonymous*; *New Light on Alcoholism*. Notice particularly the Bible material in the second chapter of 1 Corinthians. The verses there speak clearly about spiritual wisdom imparted by God, and they differentiate it from the "foolishness" that the "natural man" (one who is not-born-again) can and does receive. The verses also point out that the natural man cannot even *understand* the wisdom imparted by God because it must be "spiritually discerned." And Henrietta Seiberling often quoted this material to AAs.

Expressed in very simple terms, early AA "quiet time" involved these elements: (1) First, a decision for Christ (often called a "complete" or "real" Surrender) which enabled one to be born-again of God's spirit and thus

become one of God's children. (2) Study of the Bible.
(3) Prayer-both group and individual. (4) Use of
devotionals like *The Upper Room* and *The Runner's
Bible*. (5) Seeking God's guidance for their lives—
something God promises and can do for those who have
received the gift of the Holy Spirit and have become His
kids (See 1 Corinthians 12:1-13; Galatians 1:11-12; 1
Peter 4:10-11; James 1:5-8).

And here are the CE Quiet Hour guidelines which were
part of Dr. Bob's Christian Endeavor training as a
youngster. Even more can be found in materials by the
Rev Dr. F. B. Meyer and by the Evangelist Dwight
Moody. The CE Founder Dr. Francis Clark wrote:

> "Undoubtedly the effort that has done most to
> impress the deepest things of the Spirit of God
> upon the Christian Endeavor movement is the
> so-called 'Quiet Hour.' . . . . Because there may
> be some who read these pages who may not
> understand the inner meaning of the Quiet
> Hour, or what the old writers understand by
> 'practising the presence of God,' the writer. . .
> tries to tell his young friends just how the Quiet
> Hour may be spent. 'Our Bible is open, perhaps
> to the familiar passage which reveals the
> wondrous truth that man dwells in God, and
> God in man, as John records it. Seek to realize
> this stupendous fact, for all Scripture is a lie if it
> is not a fact. Say to yourself over and over
> again: 'God is here. God is here. God is within
> me. I am His child. God is my Father'." (Clark,
> *Christian Endeavor*, *supra*, pp. 525-26).

> "So it was proposed that those who wished
> should band themselves together in a purely
> voluntary organization called 'the Comrades of

the Quiet Hour.' The name was chosen rather than the similar name of 'The Morning Watch' in order to give the utmost freedom as to the time which should be devoted to meditation and personal communion with God, though the morning was strongly recommended. Those who became "comrades" agreed to spend fifteen minutes a day not merely in Bible-reading and petition, but in genuine personal communion with the Unseen. . . . Quiet Hour literature began to abound; 'Quiet Hours' led by some of the most eminent Christians in the land began to be held in connection with the conventions both State and national. Now more than 40,000 have been definitely enrolled. . ." (Clark, *Christian Endeavor, supra*, p. 357).

See also these Christian Endeavor writings by Francis E. Clark, *The Presence of God; Living and Loving; The Golden Alphabet; A Daily Message for Christian Endeavorers;* and *The Great Secret*; Belle M. Brain, *The Morning Watch* and *Quaint Thoughts*; J. Wilbur Chapman, *The Surrendered Life: Quiet Hour Meditations* And note that the foregoing titles were all published by United Society of Christian Endeavor. Popular also in Christian Endeavor was Brother Lawrence's *Practicing the Presence of God* and F. B. Meyer's *The Secret of Guidance*. For even further literature that AAs independently read on Quiet Time and the Morning Watch, see Dick B., *Dr. Bob and His Library; The Books Early AAs Read for Spiritual Growth*, 7th ed; *Good Morning: Quiet Time, Morning Watch, Meditation and Early A.A.;* and *Making Known the Biblical History and Roots of A.A*

The Christian Endeavor/AA Emphasis on Love and Service

There is very frequent mention in Christian Endeavor literature of the importance of love and service. And I cannot recall any similar phraseology or emphasis in the thousands of Oxford Group writings I have read and analyzed. As to the subject, Christian Endeavor's Dr. Clark wrote:

> "Christian Endeavor is a watch
> Whose mainspring is love,
> Whose movement is service.
> Whose hands point to heavenly joys on the dial
> of eternity" (Clark, *Christian Endeavor*, *supra*, p.
> 316).

The following is a relevant, succinct description of the Endeavor's position:

> **"...it is a fellowship based on a broad platform of service, love to Christ, and work for Him. On this platform all can stand."** Francs E. Clark. *World Wide Endeavor: The Story of The Young Peoples Society of Christian Endeavor, From the Beginning and In All Lands*. [Philadelphia, PA: Gillespie, Metzgar & Kelley], 1895, p. 263.

In his last, very brief, and much quoted address to AAs, Dr. Bob made the following point—seemingly springing forward from his long-held and later refreshed memory of earlier Christian Endeavor strong points:

> "Our Twelve Steps, when simmered down to the last, resolve themselves into the words 'love'

and 'service.' We understand what love is, *and we understand what service is. So let's bear those two things in mind" (DR. BOB, supra,* p. 338).

The last paragraph of A.A.'s own biographical sketch on Dr. Bob said:

"Dr. Bob firmly believed that 'love and service' are the cornerstones of Alcoholics Anonymous." *The Co-Founders of Alcoholics Anonymous: Biographical Sketches. Their Last Major Talks.* NY: Alcoholics Anonymous World Services, Inc., 1972, 1975, p. 9.

The Necessity for Believing on Jesus Christ:

The Bible makes the following very specific comments about the way to salvation, the abundant life, and everlasting life through Jesus Christ (and see John 3:1-8, 14-17; 10:9-10; 14:5-6):

"This Jesus hath God raised up, whereof we are all witnesses. . . . Therefore let all the house of Israel know assuredly, that God hath made that same Jesus, whom ye have crucified, both Lord and Christ" (Acts 2:32, 36).

"Be it known unto you all, and to all the people of Israel, that by the name of Jesus Christ of Nazareth, whom ye crucified, whom God hath raised from the dead, even by him doth this man stand before you whole. . . . Neither is there salvation in any other: for there is none other name under heaven given among men, whereby we must be saved" Acts 4:10, 12).

"That if thou shalt confess with thy mouth the
Lord Jesus, and shalt believe in thine heart that
God hath raised him from the dead, thou shalt
be saved. For with the heart man believeth unto
righteousness; and with the mouth confession is
made unto salvation. . . .For whoever shall call
upon the name of the Lord shall be saved"
(Romans 10:9-10, 13).

In early A.A., a surrender to, and decision for, Christ
was a "must"—though you'd hardly know it from
reading almost any history pertaining to Bill Wilson or
the fellowship as a whole. Yet when I was gathering
material for my Akron Genesis book, Bill Wilson's
secretary and A.A.'s first archivist Nell Wing phoned me
from New York to tell me specific pages in *DR. BOB and
the Good Oldtimers* which described the required
surrenders. But the following statements by several
A.A. Akron pioneers verify and detail the specifics of the
required early A.A. "surrender to Christ":

"They would not let you in unless you
surrendered to Jesus Christ on your knees"
(From a recorded telephone conversation with
Danny W. in Lancaster, California, from A.A.
old-timer Ed Andy of Lorain, Ohio. The
statement was made on January 9, 1993, and I
personally heard it; see also, Dick B., *The
Golden Text of A.A.*, p. 31).

"They took me upstairs to be a born again
human being and be God's helper to alcoholics"
(Letter from Larry B., A.A. old-timer from
Cleveland, Ohio to the author, dated September
18, 1992. Larry stated that this quote correctly
described his surrender; see also, Dick B., *The
Golden Text of A.A.*, p. 32).

Clarence Snyder—who came into A.A. in February of
1938 and was sponsored by Dr. Bob—   said that Doc
told him. "Young feller, it's about time you make your
full surrender.". . . At Clarence's surrender, T. Henry,
Doc, and a couple of Oxford group members went into
T. Henry's bedroom. They all, including Clarence . . .
got down on their knees in an attitude of prayer. They
all placed their hands on Clarence, and then proceeded
to pray. These people introduced Clarence to Jesus as
his Lord and Savior. They explained to Clarence that
this was First Century Christianity. Then they prayed for
a healing and removal of Clarence's sins, especially his
alcoholism" (See Mitchell K. *How It Worked*, *supra*, pp.
58, 70).

END

Appendix 3

The Two Different A.A. Root Streams

First, The Unique Christian Fellowship Program of the Akron Pioneers

Distinguishing Akron's Program from Bill's Later Twelve Steps

You will never understand the Akron program unless you look at the real picture, the whole picture, and the complete picture, of the origins, founding, principles and practices of the first years of pioneer A.A. Even those apologists for Bill Wilson, who ignore the specifics on the Akron program, seem reluctantly to concede the differences:

> Because the Twelve Steps have long been the treatment model embraced by nearly all substance-abuse treatment programs, it is hard to imagine that they could have been produced amid swirls of controversy. . . . When the project got under way, there seemed to be nearly as many programs of recovery as there were alcoholics who had recovered. . . . Getting agreement on the book itself was even harder. Francis Hartigan, *Bill W: A Biography of Alcoholics Anonymous Cofounder Bill Wilson*. NY: St. Martin's Press, 2000, p. 114.

Hartigan's book is no more enlightening about the *differences* than any of the other contemporary histories. But it calls to mind again Dr. Bob's emphatic statement that he did not write the Twelve Steps and, in fact, had nothing to do with the writing of them.

Another writer observed:

> Although the breadth of A.A.'s varieties is a new phenomenon, the reality of diversity within Alcoholics Anonymous is not merely recent. A.A.'s differences were one reason why it developed in so decentralized a fashion. Early researchers were aware of that, but they fell into the easy (and enduring) trap of researching what was available - studying those A.A.s who welcomed their research. Influenced also by the secularization hypothesis shared by most sociologists of the era, they tended to overlook the Akron birthplace of A.A. and its more Oxford Group-oriented offspring, concentrating their attention on New York A.A. and its derivatives. Ernest Kurtz, *The Collected Ernie Kurtz.*, WV: The Bishop of Books, 1997, p. 4.

The Influence on Bill of His own Heritage and Early Experiences

In point of a time line as to beginning, the first part of the A.A. picture has to do with New York. The New York story goes like this: Rowland Hazard treated for alcoholism with Dr. Carl Jung, went back to drinking, returned to Jung for an answer, and was told that his plight was hopeless unless he had a conversion. Jung recommended Rowland seek a religious association.

Rowland became involved with the Oxford Group and became thoroughly familiar with its literature, principles, and practices. Rowland was cured. Then he and two other Oxford Group friends sought ought Ebby Thacher, an alcoholic who was about to be institutionalized for alcoholism. The judge turned Ebby over to Rowland's care. Rowland taught Ebby the Oxford Group precepts and placed Ebby at Calvary Rescue Mission which was run by Rev. Sam Shoemaker's Calvary Episcopal Church in New York. There Ebby made a decision for Christ. He quit drinking. In turn, Ebby sought out his alcoholic friend Bill Wilson, and told Bill of his own cure. Bill then went to Calvary Rescue Mission seeking what Ebby had. Bill was drunk, but made his own decision for Christ at an altar call. Though drinking, he soon proclaimed he had been "born again." Bill checked in to Towns Hospital one more time and told the staff he had "found something." Later, Bill talked to Ebby at Towns some more about the Oxford Group program, surrendered to God "as Bill then understood God," and had his "hot flash" experience which he believed to be his finding of God. The experience could simply have been an hallucination. But Bill felt its reality was validated by his doctor's telling him he was not crazy, and by his reading William James' accounts of "religious experiences." Whatever that experience amounted to in reality, it marked an end to Bill's drinking. Bill set out to help other drunks, but had no success whatever. The reason seems fairly obvious to me. Bill was a fervent messenger, but he had no real message. Bill had been a self-proclaimed "conservative atheist." He married a non-Christian woman of Swedenborgian persuasion and married her in a Swedenborgian Church. She outspokenly claimed she needed no "conversion." For his part, Bill had never read the Bible. He had never belonged to a church. His secretary told me that he had never read much at all, not then, nor in later years, concerning things like the Oxford Group and Shoemaker literature. And with six or less months of sobriety, he was hardly capable of expounding capably or persuasively the Oxford Group or Bible ideas later to be incorporated into his own Big Book manuscript and the Twelve Steps.

The Very Different Akron Heritage and Experiences

The picture in Akron was totally different. Dr. Bob's whole early family life had centered around church–the North Congregational Church in Vermont. Also in the burgeoning youth movement known as the Christian Endeavor Society which had a group in his church. And perhaps even in the St. Johnsbury Academy he attended. At the church and Christian Endeavor activities, Bob was soaked in conversion meetings, prayer meetings, Bible study, Quiet Hours, Christian fellowship, confessions of Christ, and Christian love and service. And despite the recently concocted stories about Bob's not being a Christian, he himself never lost his status as a born-again child of God, nor did he forget the soaking–especially in his later years when he so badly needed help and wanted to help others by utilizing the training he had received. Bob continued his Christian church affiliations throughout his life. He took his kids to Christian Sunday Schools. When he joined the Oxford Group, he dived back into the Bible, read it three times, and devoured Christian and Oxford Group literature of the day. Once he had achieved the sobriety that sprang from his association with Bill Wilson, he gave the Bible, Christianity, and Christian fellowship a full bore shot.

In their intense discussions in the summer of 1935 at the Smith home, Bob and Bill talked Bible, Bible, Bible. They listened to Bible, Bible, Bible. And they developed a special interest in the Book of James, Jesus's Sermon on the Mount, and 1 Corinthians 13. These three Bible segments were to form the basis for Akron's program and success. And I have pointed out their elements in several different writings, including this instant one, as well as *The Good Book and The Big Book: A.A.'s Roots in the Bible*; *The Akron Genesis of Alcoholics Anonymous*; *Why Early A.A. Succeeded*; *When Early AAs Were Cured and Why*; *Twelve Steps for You*; and two articles on A.A.'s roots in the three Bible segments. See: http://www.dickb.com/AAsJamesClub.shtml; and http://www.dickb.com/AAbasicideas.shtml

Without doubt, the heart and significance of these fundamental early Akron A.A. Christian touchstones of recovery still remain a virtual unknown to most A.A. members today. By one method or another, whether because of ridicule, intimidation, or suppression, today's AAs simply never get close to the real story.

The additional importance of contrasting the Oxford Group experiences in Akron with Bill Wilson's brief Oxford Group membership and activities in New York

Unlike the Oxford Group itself–the Oxford Group in which Wilson had cut his teeth on the East Coast— *Akron's* "alcoholic squad" was focused on helping drunks. It insisted on abstinence–which the Oxford Group didn't. It insisted on early hospitalization–which was not a part of Oxford Group work. It required confession of Christ–again not an Oxford Group prerequisite. It stressed Bible study and prayer–which were really less important in the Oxford Group than its "life-changing" work, international teams, and world-changing mission.

Akron's alcoholic squad conducted "old fashioned prayer meetings"–which was a moniker never applied to Oxford Group meetings or house parties. It held almost continuous fellowship meetings in the Akron homes and called itself a Christian Fellowship–not the Oxford Group's "A First Century Christian Fellowship" or "Moral Re-Armament." For a decade, the Akron pioneers carried the message of *cure* by conducting daily visits to newcomers in the hospital. Two Oxford Group ideas did, however, achieve major prominence in Akron. One was a staunch adherence to the Four Absolutes (from *Principles of Jesus* by Robert Speer), and the other was the elimination of sin from one's life (which was an Oxford Group focus but most assuredly the focus of the Bible as well, and—in the Bible—a focus with far greater insistence, intensity and detail).

What the Akron Pioneers Learned and Did

Finding the Drunk

Their first prerequisite was finding a real, "seemingly hopeless, "medically incurable" drunk. Henrietta Seiberling was the first to aid in the quest by rooting Bob out of his "secret drinking" hole and praying for the solution that turned up with Bill's visit. Bill's own searches in the hospitals, missions, and meetings in the New York area provided guidance as to where and how to search.

The Usual Hospitalization

Next, in Akron Dr. Bob and some pioneers would often meet with the newcomer drunk and his family to get the lay of the land. Most of the time, the alcoholic was immediately hospitalized. Dr. Bob visited him every day and frequently talked to him for hours. Then other pioneers would visit, share their experience, and tell the newcomer that help was on the way. At the end of five to seven days, Dr. Bob would visit. He'd ask if the drunk believed in God; and, if that new person did, that patient was asked to get down on his knees and pray with Dr. Bob. This was the man's "first" surrender.

Home Fellowships

Next, many of the drunks were taken from the hospital into the Smith home. Later into the homes of others such as Wally G. and his wife, Tom Lucas and his wife, Clarence Snyder and his wife, and others. Wherever they were housed–in their own home or in the homes of others–the drunks would congregate at the Smith home at the crack of dawn to hear Anne Smith lead them in prayer, Bible study, seeking guidance, and discussing the items she shared from her journal. During each day, there were frequent fellowships, phone calls, visits from Henrietta, visits with Bob and Anne, as well as individual Bible study, reading, and prayer.

"Regular" Meetings

Mondays saw a set up meeting where, with God's guidance, a leader and topic were selected for the

Wednesday meeting. The "regular" meeting on Wednesday was an Oxford Group meeting of sorts. But it was sufficiently different from regular Oxford Group activities that it was appropriate called a "clandestine lodge" [secret lodge] of the Oxford Group; and its format was really that of the Christian Endeavor groups of Dr. Bob's youth. Meetings opened with prayer. Next, there was invariably reading from the Bible. Next group prayers, followed by a brief quiet time for guidance. There would be a discussion of some Bible topic or other matter applicable to their new lives. Sometimes the topic would concern an idea in the Bible and sometimes a topic drawn from one of the devotionals like *The Upper Room* or *My Utmost for His Highest.* The discussion would usually be led by Henrietta, Dr. Bob, or T. Henry. Later, in the program's development, Anne Smith would share from the Bible or her journal.

The "Real" Surrenders

At that point and during the Wednesday meeting, new members were taken upstairs to T. Henry's bedroom where two or three would pray over and with them individually after the manner of James 5:16. The new person was led to accept Christ, to ask that alcohol be taken out of his life, and then to declare that he would live by the principles of the Four Absolutes. It is undisputed that, at these "real surrenders," as they were often called, the newcomer accepted Christ as his Lord and Saviour, became born again of the spirit of God, and emerged as one of God's kids.

The Afterglow

Downstairs again. Dr. Bob would recruit old-timers to join in visiting the hospitalized newcomers. The regular meeting closed with the Lord's Prayer and was followed by socializing. There was Christian and other Oxford Group literature on the table in T. Henry's furnace room; and it was taken or swapped by members. There were no steps. There was no Big Book or basic text other than what Dr. Bob's son called "God's Big Book"— the Bible. There were no drunkalogs. There appeared to be no formal observance of Oxford Group procedures like confession, conviction, and restitution. There is evidence that, at later points, Dr. Bob would meet with a newcomer, review his sins and shortcomings, and pray with him to have them taken away. And always, there was individual Bible reading, reading of literature, prayer, seeking of guidance, and use individually and in meetings of daily devotionals like *The Upper Room, The Runner's Bible,* and *Victorious Living*. None of these devotionals could be called an Oxford Group book or pamphlet.

It was all just that simple in Akron. Find a drunk. Hospitalize the drunk. Share with him there that there was hope and victory available at his own option. Confirm his belief in God, then leading him to surrender to Christ. Envelope him in a fellowship where he was taught Bible and Christian principles, prayed, and provided counseling from non-alcoholic Christian "teachers" like T. Henry, Henrietta, and Anne Smith.

Repetition. Repetition. Repetition. Three Bible segments–James, the Sermon, and 1 Corinthians 13– were the absolutely essential Akron elements. And that's why this particular title has been written. The three Bible parts provided the basic ideas for the Akron successes and later even to portions of the Big Book Steps. And the newcomer had help, lots of it, in hearing, understanding, and applying what was studied. Henrietta, Anne, Bob, and Mr. and Mrs. Williams were all highly intelligent, well-educated *teachers.* They knew their Bible. They knew their Oxford Group. They knew their Christian precepts. They knew their Christian literature. And they practiced what they preached. Yes. Preached! They preached the good news—the Gospel.

Moreover, the newcomer was specifically urged to study for himself, to read the books that Dr. Bob circulated, to report later to Dr. Bob on just what they had read and learned, and to use the devotionals that were given to, or made available to him. The newcomer thus did have teachers. He did have text books. The first "text-book" was "God's Big Book," as Dr. Bob's son used to refer to the Bible. Others included the wide range of devotionals, Christian writings, and Oxford Group materials then available. See Dick B., *The Books Early AAs Read for Spiritual Growth, 7th ed; Dr. Bob and His Library;* and *Anne Smith's Journal* for specifics.

That Akron scene was much much different from the New York situation where there is little evidence the Bible was studied at all by AAs—and certainly not by Bill himself said exactly that. The East Coast Oxford Group meetings were acceptable to Bill for only a short time period—though the "clandestine lodge" continued in Akron for at least five years. And we have uncovered little evidence that, on the East Coast, either Christian literature or Anne's Journal were much read, if at all.

If you understand the points just made, you'll appreciate better my emphasis on the practically unknown early Akron program, its successes, and the cures it rightly claimed. Whatever their particular religious or irreligious views, that is an historical picture which should be known to every Twelve Step person and group today. And certainly to those who are attempting to treat or help them.

END

Appendix 4

Background on the Bible's Book of James and James the "Author"

By now, it should be very clear to the reader that James was the favorite part of the Bible for A.A. pioneers. It should also be clear that they wanted the name "James" for their society. Therefore, it seems important to review some of the background for this unique book of the Bible.

James the Brother of Jesus of Nazareth

Which "James"?: You could ask a hundred people in Alcoholics Anonymous, or any "12-Step Fellowship" if they know who "James" was, or if they had heard in A.A. about the "James Club," or if they had ever heard about the relationship of the Bible's Book of James to Alcoholics Anonymous. The chances are you would draw a blank with most, if not all those questioned. Yet there's lots to be told and much to be learned, all to the good of those who want what early AAs claimed and had a cure for their alcoholism. When we speak of "James," we first are speaking of the person or persons named as *James* in the Good Book. In fact, we are speaking only of the "James" mentioned in the New Testament.

And this appendix will cover what the Bible and the work of some Bible scholars tells us. But there is a *caveat:* If the Bible itself doesn't actually provide a specific answer, then the remarks of the scholars are frequently speculations or educated guessing. Hence we don't always know for sure that we have the correct answers.

The Many Named James: There are several persons named James who are mentioned in the New Testament. See *New Bible Dictionary*, 2d ed. England: Inter-Varsity Press, 1982, pp. 549-550.

(1) There is *James, the son of Zebedee*, a Galilean fisherman who was called with his brother John to be one of Jesus's twelve apostles. Thus Matthew 4:21-22, speaking of Jesus, says: "And going on from thence, he saw other two brethren, James the son of Zebedee, and John his brother, in a ship with Zebedee their father, mending their nets; and he called them. And they immediately left the ship and their father, and followed him."

(2). There is *James, the son of Alphaeus*, another of the twelve apostles. Thus Matthew10:2-4 says: "Now the names of the twelve apostles are these; The first, Simon, who is called Peter, and Andrew his brother; James the son of Zebedee and John his brother; Philip, and Bartholemew; Thomas and Matthew the publican; *James the son of Alphaeus*, and Lebaeus, whose surname was Thaddaeus; Simon the Canaanite, and Judas Iscariot, who also betrayed him (italics added).

(3) There may be an *otherwise unknown James* who was the brother of the apostle Judas (not Iscariot). See Luke 6:16; Acts 1:13. But here is no uniform agreement on this point.

(4) Then there is James, the brother of Jesus. This James is specifically referred to in the Bible as the Lord's brother. Matthew 13:55 states: "Is not this [Jesus] the carpenter's son? Is not his mother called Mary? *And his brethren, James*, and Joses, and Simon, and Judas?" (italics added). The Apostle Paul writes in Galatians 1:18-19: "Then after three years I went up to Jerusalem to see Peter, and abode with him fifteen days. But other of the apostles saw I none, save *James the Lord's brother*." (italics added)

James, the brother of Jesus, was not one of the Twelve Apostles.

The Lord's Brother James was not until after the resurrection a believer, and did not, until Jesus was raised, honor his brother Jesus. John 7:5 states:

> For neither did his brethren believe in him.

Mark 6:3-7 states:

> Is not this the carpenter [Jesus], the son of Mary, the brother of James, and Joses, and of Juda, and Simon? And are not his sisters here with us? And they were offended at him. But Jesus said unto them, A prophet is not without honour, but in his own country, and among his own kin, and in his own house. And he could there do no mighty work, save that he laid his hands upon a few sick folk, and healed them. And he marveled because of their unbelief. And he went round about the villages, teaching. And he called unto him the twelve, and began to send them forth by two and two; and gave them power over unclean spirits. See also Philip

Schaff, *History of the Christian Church, Volume I*, 3rd ed. Grand Rapids, MI: Wm. B. Eerdman's Publishing Company, 1910, pp. 265-66, 503.

This brother James is mentioned with frequency in the Bible. And numerous scholars have referred to him as "the brother of our Lord." See F. F. Bruce. *The New Testament Documents: Are They Reliable?* Grand Rapids, MI: William B. Eerdmans Publishing Co., 5th ed., 1983, pp. 11, 106, 112; *The Companion Bible: Being The Authorized Version of 1611 with Structures and Critical and Explanatory Note with 198 Appendices*. Grand Rapids, MI: Zondervan Bible Publishers, 1974, p. 1847, Appendix 182, p. 205; *The Elesiastical History of Eusebius Pamphilus, Bishop of Cesarea, in Palestine*, Grand Rapids, MI: Baker Book House, 1981, pp. 48-49, 75-76, 289). See also the other authorities cited in this Part of our article.

After the resurrection of Jesus, James, the Lord's Brother, Had a New Role

God raised Jesus from the dead. The Gospels and Acts reported that Jesus was resurrected and seen by many. The Apostle Peter twice confirmed that he and others had seen Jesus after he had been resurrected. Acts 2:32 states: "This Jesus hath God raised up, whereof we are all witnesses." Acts 5:30 states: "The God of our fathers raised up Jesus, whom ye slew and hanged on a tree."

Things changed for James after God raised Jesus from the dead.

First, following the resurrection, Jesus was seen in his resurrected body by James and by all the apostles. In 1 Corinthians 15:3-7, Paul wrote:

> For I delivered unto you first of that which I also received, how that Christ died   for   our   sins according to the scriptures; And that he was buried, and that he rose again the third day according to the scriptures; And that he was seen of Cephas, then of the twelve: After that he was seen of above five hundred brethren at once; of whom the greater part remain unto this present, but some are fallen asleep. After that, he was seen of James; then of all the apostles. See also Bruce, *New Testament History, supra,* pp. 211, 244; *New Bible Dictionary, supra,* p. 550.

Second, historians report that James had then converted and begun keeping company with the twelve apostles. See *Eusebius Elesiastical History, supra,* 75; also, according to Acts 1:13 and other frequent references to James, he thereafter kept regular company with the twelve apostles. See Schaff, *History of the Christian Church, supra,* p. 266; Bruce, *New Testament History, supra,* pp. 210-211.

Third, before long, James seemed to have become a leader of the Jewish-Christian church at Jerusalem. In Galatians 1:17-19, Paul writes that, after his (Paul's) own conversion:

> Neither went I up to Jerusalem to them which were apostles before me . . . Then after three years I went up to Jerusalem to see Peter, and abode with him fifteen days. But other of the

apostles saw I none, save James the Lord's brother.

Fourteen years later, Paul returned to Jerusalem with Barnabus. He wrote in Galatians 2:9:

> And when James, Cephas, and John, who seemed to be pillars, perceived the grace that was given unto me, they gave to me and Barnabus the right hands of fellowship; that we should go unto the heathen, and they unto the circumcision. See also Acts 12:17; *Eusebius Ecclesiastical History, supra,* p. 49.

Fourth, James allegedly became the leader of the Jerusalem church and then was killed. Though the remarks are undocumented in Scripture, some scholars state that James remained as sole leader of the Jerusalem church, working to maintain its unity with Paul and his mission when Paul visited Jerusalem for the last time (*New Bible Dictionary, supra,* p. 550). And that, a few years later, James suffered martyrdom by stoning at the instigation of the high priest Ananus (Schaff, *History of the Christian Church, supra,* p. 221, 267-268, 276-277).

Many scholars, without citing Scriptural authority, named the Lord's brother, "James the Just." They wrote also that he became the bishop of Jerusalem.

Hegesippus' largely legendary tradition claims that James was known as "the Just" because of his (Jewish) piety. Whatever the reason, he is said by many Bible scholars to be, and to have been specifically named, "James the Just" Schaff. *History of the Christian Church, supra*, pp. 264-677; F. F. Bruce, *New Testament History*. New York: Doubleday-Galilee, 1980, pp. 94, 200, 205, 225, 347, 349, 375, 391; Adolph Harnack. *The Expansion of Christianity in the First Three Centuries*, Vol. I. Eugene, OR: Wipf and Stock Publishers, 1998, pp. 50-51, 92; Henry Chadwick, *The Early Church*, NY: Penguin Books, 1967, p. 18; *Eusebius Ecclesiastical History, supra*, pp. ii-iv, 49, 76. At page 76 Eusebius says: "But James, the brother of the Lord, who, as there were many by this name, was surnamed the Just by all, from the days of our Lord until now, received the government of the church with the apostles."

Some scholars have claimed that James was appointed the first bishop of Jerusalem and, according to tradition, by the Lord himself (*New Bible Dictionary, supra*, p. 550). Moreover, that he probably presided over a council of the apostles and elders of the church at Jerusalem and gave their judgment (See Acts 15:13-23; *New Bible Dictionary, supra*, p. 550).

James, Confession, and Prayers for the Sick

The Special Importance to AAs of the Statements by James, in Chapter Five of the Book of James: Of major significance to AAs concerned with their early history and the cures in the pioneer A.A. period is the impact on the early A.A. fellowship of James 5:13-16. And we will discuss this in the next part of this article.

James wrote about two important ideas:

(1) Confession of sins. James 5:16 states: "Confess your faults one to another."

(2) Prayers by the elders of the church for a sick person, accompanied by anointing with oil. James 5:13-16 states:

> Is any among you afflicted? Let him pray. Is any merry? Let him sing psalms. Is any sick among you? let him call for the elders of the church; and let them pray over him, anointing him with oil in the name of the Lord: And the prayer of faith shall save the sick, and the Lord shall raise him up; and if he have committed sins, they shall be forgiven him. Confess your faults one to another, and pray one for another, that ye may be healed. The effectual fervent prayer of a righteous man availeth much.

Both ideas confession to another, and prayers for the sick became of substantial importance in early A.A. surrenders, and later even in some practices of the Fifth Step of A.A.'s Big Book. In fact, the whole A.A. process of surrender in Akron whether at the hospital or later "upstairs" at the home of Dr. Bob or that of T. Henry Williams involved several of the surrender, prayer, confession, forgiveness, and healing ideas in the Book of James. These spilled over into early A.A. And the practices themselves had produced, for hundreds of centuries (those after which there had been the remission of sins and other accomplishments of Jesus) healing work by the Apostolic and later churches. See Rev. F.W. Puller, *Anointing of the Sick in Scripture and Tradition with Some Consideration of the Numbering of the Sacraments* (London: Society For Promoting Christian Knowledge, 1904); J. R. Pridie, *The*

Church"s Ministry of Healing (London: Society For Promoting Christian Knowledge, 1926), pp. 67-86, 123-134; and Dick B., *When Early AAs Were Cured. And Why* (Kihei, HI: Paradise Research Publications, Inc., 2003), pp. 89-101. They are still employed in A.A. by many of the followers of A.A. pioneer Clarence Snyder and his third wife, Grace. See Dick B., *That Amazing Grace: The Role of Clarence and Grace S. in Alcoholics Anonymous*. San Rafael, CA: Paradise Research Publications, 1996, pp. 7, 16, 26-28, 34-38, 83-87, 92-93, 95-106, 113-14; Three Clarence Snyder Sponsee Old-timers and Their Wives. Compiled and edited by Dick B. *Our A.A. Legacy to the Faith Community: A Twelve-Step Guide for Those Who Want to Believe*. FL: Came to Believe Publications, 2005, pp. 5, 99-100.

The Belated Status of the Book of James as Part of New Testament Canon

The Dispute Over the Book: For many decades during the First Century and even thereafter, the Book of James was questioned and disputed by some. See James J. Megivern, *Bible Interpretation: Official Catholic Teachings*. Wilmington, NC: A Consortium Book, 1978, p. 27; *New Bible Dictionary, supra,* p. 175) For several centuries, it was not accepted in the canon of authoritative New Testament books. See Bruce, *The New Testament Documents, supra*, pp. 21-23; J. N. D. Kelly, *Early Christian Doctrines*, 2d ed. New York: Harper & Row Publishers, pp. 59-60; *New Bible Dictionary, supra*, pp. 171-177.

Its Acceptance in the Fourth Century: In 367 A.D., Athanasius, Bishop of Alexandria, laid down the twenty-seven books of our New Testament as alone canonical; with Jerome and Augustine following his example shortly thereafter in the West. The Book of James was included (See Megivern, *Bible Interpretation*, *supra*, pp. 36-38, 48, 65-66). The process farther east took a little longer (Bruce, *The New Testament Documents*, *supra*, pp. 25-26).

The Problems that Arose from Disputes about "Faith" and "Works"

Arguments persist to this day as to whether James and his "faith without works" teaching is in conflict with Paul's doctrine of "justification by faith."

There really are two separate ideas involved:

(1) Righteousness freedom from sin that righteousness, justification, redemption, and freedom from sin and condemnation which comes as a gift to believers by reason of their acceptance of Jesus Christ as Lord and Saviour Romans 3:21-30; 4:23-25; 6; 8; 10:8-10; and by reason of the sacrifice made by Jesus in payment for their sins. Thus Romans 3:27-28 states: "Where is boasting then? It is excluded. By what law? Of works? Nay: but by the law of faith. Therefore we conclude that a man is justified by faith without the deeds of the law".

(2) The practice of the love of God fulfilling the royal law according to Scripture: "Thou shalt love thy neighbor as thyself." James 2:8 states: "If ye fulfil the royal law according to the scripture, Thou shalt love thy

neighbor as thyself, ye do well." See also Matthew 22:36-40; 1 Corinthians 13; 1 John 3:11, 23; 4:11, 20; 2 John 4; Galatians 5:14.

Righteousness from The faith of Jesus Christ not "works" or "the deeds of the law"-justifies [acquits] those who choose to become Christians (Romans 3:20-24 states:

> Therefore by the deeds of the law there shall no flesh be justified in his sight. . . But now the righteousness of God without the law is manifested. . . . Even the righteousness of God which is by faith of Jesus Christ unto all and upon all them that believe: for there is no difference. For all have sinned and come short of the glory of God; Being justified freely by his grace through the redemption that is in Christ Jesus. . . . Therefore we conclude that a man is justified by faith without the deeds of the law.

This is the faith of Jesus Christ who was delivered for the offenses of believers, was raised again for their justification, and whose redeeming sacrifice acquits them of sin. Romans 4:24-5:1 states:

> But for us also to whom it [righteousness] shall be imputed, if we believe on him that raised up Jesus our Lord from the dead; Who was delivered for our offenses, and was raised again for our justification. Therefore being justified by faith, we have peace with God through our Lord Jesus Christ.

Believers are then said to be free from the dominion or rulership of sin. Romans 6:14, 22 state:

> For sin shall not have dominion over you: for ye
> are not under the law, but under grace. . . . But
> now being made free from sin, and become
> servants to God, ye have your fruit unto
> holiness, and the end everlasting life.

The righteous, acquitted believer can therefore stand before God without any sense of guilt, shame, or condemnation. Romans 8:1-2, 33 state:

> There is therefore now no condemnation to
> them which are in Christ Jesus. . . For the law of
> the Spirit of life in Christ Jesus hath made me
> free from the law of sin and death. . . . Who
> shall lay any thing to the charge of God's elect.
> It is God that justifieth.

What is the significance of this righteousness which comes, by grace, to the sons of God?

The point is that, at the time of his acceptance of Christ and salvation, the believer need no longer walk about with the hangdog feeling of guilt. He has been cleansed by the blood Jesus Christ shed for him. He has been bought with a price – the price of the life of God's only begotten son. And that salvation by grace – the unearned freedom – is what makes the believer a free person who needs to do nothing more to achieve God's approval. Yet the problem is given a different twist in 12 Step fellowships who seem to have overlooked "by the grace of God" in their talk. A.A. is shot full of references to "by the grace of God." Yet its member seldom hears how that grace is manifested so that—if that member, like the pioneer AAs, chooses to become a born again Christian--he need not run about continuing to confess shame, guilt, and self-condemnation. In fact, it seems to be big deal today to continue to feature guilt and shame as problems for the newcomer. And to indicate that therapy or treatment are required to bring freedom and release. But a believer's freedom and release can and will come from faith not by taking some steps or by engaging in some "works" that he must "do" to become "good," be "free," and only then be acquitted of his sin.

Paul wrote in Galatians 5:1: "Stand fast therefore in the liberty wherewith Christ hath made us free, and be not entangled again with the yoke of bondage."

There is an additional point having to do with "works" or living in obedience to God's will and Christ's teachings. That is the lesson to be learned from a study of James and the phrase "faith without works is dead."

Practicing the law of love in God's commandments, and the obedience involved in "doing" good works. James and other New Testament scriptures add the warning that faith, justification, and righteousness should not be barren or alone or leave the believer static. He has work to do. He is to be a "doer of the word." He is to "do" the will of His father. And James teaches that faith alone does not bear fruit unless accompanied by the love of God in the renewed mind in manifestation (See James, Chapter 2, 1 Corinthians, Chapter 13). James leaves no doubt about the need for obedience to the commandments of God, the importance of God's Word, and the love of God and Jesus Christ. In addition, on the subject of works or deeds, James simply spells out much in conformity with the Sermon on the Mount and 1 Corinthians 13 just what faith means *in practice*.

***On the one hand, faith empowers. On the other
hand, Obedience implements.*** In the Book of Acts,
Peter said of the man who had been healed of being
lame since birth:

> And when they had set them in the midst, they
> asked, By what power or by what name have
> you done this? Then Peter, filled with the Holy
> Ghost, said unto them, Ye rulers of the people
> and elders of Israel, If we this day be examined
> of the good deed done to the impotent man, by
> what means he is made whole; Be it known
> unto you all, and to all the people of Israel, that
> by the name of Jesus Christ of Nazareth whom
> ye crucified, whom God raised from the dead,
> even by him doth this man stand here before
> you whole (Acts 4:7-10).

The faith of Jesus Christ empowers. In Acts 1:8, Jesus
told the assembled just before he was taken up from
them into heaven: "But ye shall receive power after that
the Holy Ghost is come upon you: and ye shall be
witnesses unto me. . ." And those men certainly did
receive that power when the day of Pentecost was fully
come (See Acts, Chapters 2 and 3). But obedience to
God was necessarily to be involved in their ensuing
deeds. In Acts 2:8, Peter began witnessing. In Acts
2:42, all "continued stedfastly in the apostles' doctrine.
. ." In Acts 4:15-20, the council threatened the
apostles, telling them they were not to speak at all nor
teach in the name of Jesus. But Peter replied, "we
cannot but speak the things which we have seen and
heard." And they all lifted up their voice to God and
asked that He grant unto them "that with all boldness
they may speak thy word"—and the place was shaken
and they were all filled with the Holy Ghost and spoke

the Word of God with boldness (Acts 4:24-31).
Obedience is to follow receipt of power. Romans 12:1-2
often cited by early AAs states:

> I beseech you therefore, brethren, by the
> mercies of God, that ye present your bodies a
> living sacrifice, holy, acceptable unto God,
> which is your reasonable service. And be not
> conformed to this world: but be ye transformed
> by the renewing of your mind, that ye may
> prove what is that good, and acceptable, and
> perfect, will of God.

I therefore believe: *There are convincing arguments
that Paul's writings on "justification by faith" establish
that a person becomes righteous on the basis of faith
alone.* This means, for example, justification—acquittal
of guilt and condemnation--has nothing to do with
legalistic observances commanded by the *Torah* (See
also David H. Stern, *Jewish New Testament
Commentary*, 6th ed. Maryland: Jewish New Testament
Publications, Inc., 1999, pp. 730-735; *Complete Jewish
Bible*, Maryland: Jewish New Testament Publications,
Inc., 1998, pp. 1511-1512).

I also believe: *There are equally convincing arguments
that James' statements consistently, harmoniously, and
correctly teach that "genuine" faith (as some scholars
refer to it) is to be implemented through obeying God's
commandments.* Some of these commandments are
certainly mentioned in James and describe various
forms of "good works" that constitute walking in love in
obedience to God's will. Paul writes in Ephesians 5:1:
"Be ye therefore followers of God as dear children; And
walk in love, as Christ also hath loved us. . ."

These points convince me of two principles: (1) "Genuine" faith comes through an outward confession of Christ and an inward acknowledgement that salvation, the new birth, faith, and the new man in Christ are based on believing and are received by grace (2 Corinthians 4:5-7, 13, 15-16; 5:17; Galatians 2:16-21; 5:6-7; Ephesians 2:1-10, 213). (2) By manifesting God's love flowing outward in the form of good works, you prove the worth and importance of faith by expressing your faith through good works good works enabled and empowered by faith, and deeds spelled out by God in Scripture that tells us what deeds constitute obedience to His will.

Comments on a New Birth by Grace, contrasted with the Doing of Works That Constitute Obedience by those who are born again

The Bible sequence that places James in perspective: We first become Christians by believing. Then we become obedient Christians by putting on the mind of Christ and becoming doers of the Word.

Saint Augustine suggested, we are not born Christians; we must become Christians. For the Protestant, the new birth comes from a decision that Jesus Christ shall be his Lord and Saviour, after which he becomes a Christian. But becoming Christians does not equate with behaving as Christians.

Children of God by Faith: The First General Epistle of John states: "Whosoever shall confess that Jesus is the Son of God, God dwelleth in him, and he in God" (1 John 4:13) and "Whosoever believeth that Jesus is the Christ is born of God. . ." (1 John 5:1). Galatians 3:23-25 states: "Wherefore the law was our schoolmaster to bring us unto Christ, that we might be justified by faith. . . .

For ye are all the children of God by faith in Christ Jesus."
See also Ephesians 1:12-13; 2:8-9; and Romans 10:8-10.

The new birth has been made available to us and is
received by the faith of Jesus Christ. Galatians 2:16
states: "Knowing that a man is not justified by the
works of the law, but by the faith of Jesus Christ, that
we might be justified by the faith of Christ."

Obedience to God by doing God's Word: James
possibly writing at an early time in terms of the New
Testament literature was simply teaching that faith
alone faith without works is dead, or barren, or idle.
See *The Companion Bible, supra*, p. 1850, note 20.
James spells out many deeds or Aworks" that are
consistent with faith, obedient to God's commandments,
and an implementation of God's law by the living of
Christian love and service the very subject about which
A.A.' s Dr. Bob spoke so simply at the close of his life.

**James emphasizes doing the will of the Father
just as does the Sermon on the Mount**. James
specifically teaches:

> For the wrath of man worketh not the
> righteousness of God. Wherefore lay apart all
> filthiness and superfluity of naughtiness, and
> receive with meekness the engrafted word,
> which is able to save your souls. But be ye
> doers of the word, and not hearers only,
> deceiving your own selves. (James 1:20-22).

The Bible states countless times that man's ways are
not God's ways. God's ways are spelled out in His Word.

These specified ways are to be obeyed by doing, lest, as James says, we deceive ourselves. Lest we wrongfully believe we are walking in love just because we have heard a way taught and believe it's a good idea. Yet we frequently idle in doing the thing that God commanded be done. As covered below, the Book of James was said to be written before Paul's epistles. James does not appear to reject the later writings and doctrines of Paul that salvation, and the new birth taught by Jesus in John, Chapter Three, come only through believing not through works or obedience of the law.

Jesus and the Apostles emphasized the need to come to God first, through believing.

John 3:3 states: "Jesus answered, and said unto him [Nicodemus], Verily, verily, I say unto thee, Except a man be born again, he cannot see the kingdom of God." John 3:16-18 states:

> For God so loved the world, that he gave his only begotten Son, that whosoever believeth in him should not perish, but have everlasting life. For God sent not his Son into the world to condemn the world; but that the world through him might be saved. He that believeth on him is not condemned; but he that believeth not is condemned already, because he hath not believed in the name of the only begotten Son of God.

The Apostle Peter wrote of Christ in 1 Peter 1:21-23 as follows:

> Who by him do believe in God, that raised him up from the dead, and gave him glory; that

> your faith and hope might be in God. Seeing ye
> have purified your souls in obeying the truth
> through the Spirit unto unfeigned love of the
> brethren, see that ye love one another with a
> pure heart fervently. Being born again, not of
> corruptible seed, but of incorruptible, by the
> word of God, which liveth and abideth forever.

The incorruptible seed of Christ, received by believing
the word of God, brings about a new birth. That new
birth comes by believing that Word, and not by doing
any or all of the Agood works" in "unfeigned love of the
brethren" which the Word does command of God's
children. As Paul wrote: "So then faith cometh by
hearing, and hearing by the word of God" (Romans
10:17).

Faith and a new birth. Followed by Works that are
fruitful when done in obedience to God's
commands.

Works do not produce faith or a new birth; nor did
James claim they did. Believing according to scripture
produces a new birth; then the believer is to follow the
two great commandments to love God and love his
neighbor. These commandments necessarily mean that
he be a doer of the word (the commandments), not a
hearer only.

The Major Lesson in the Book of James

It has become a simple matter for some to equate the
teachings in James (and, for that matter, in the Sermon
on the Mount and 1 Corinthians 13) with teaching
people how to "be good Christians" and how to "do

good Christian works." But this erroneous processing was noticed and criticized in some of the very books early AAs studied. Two very popular and respected writers—studied at some length by A.A. pioneers—spelled out the real significance of "living by the principles of the Sermon on the Mount."

One writer, Oswald Chambers, warned of placing Jesus as Teacher first, instead of Saviour. It is the new birth, said Chambers, that changes us and empowers us to follow the demanding teachings of the Lord Jesus. In his title, *Studies in the Sermon on the Mount* (London: Simpkin Marshall, Ltd.), Chambers wrote at page i:

> Beware of placing our Lord as Teacher first instead of as Saviour. That tendency is prevalent today, and it is a dangerous tendency. We must know Him first as Saviour before His teaching has any meaning for us, or before it has any meaning other than an ideal which leads us to despair. . . . If Jesus is only a Teacher, then all He can do is to tantalize us by erecting a standard we cannot come anywhere near. But if we know Him first as Saviour, by being born again from above, we know that He did not come to teach us only. He came to make us what He teaches we should be. The Sermon on the Mount is a statement of the life we will live when the Holy Spirit is having His way with us.

The other writer, E. Stanley Jones, pointed up that the new birth, standing alone, though empowering, means little if it does not incorporate in that birth the attributes that Jesus taught. In speaking of the receipt of the Holy Spirit on Pentecost [described in Acts 2], Jones wrote in

The Christ of the Mount: A Working Philosophy of Life
(NY: The Abingdon Press, 1931), at page 18:

> Pentecost had the content of the Sermon on the
> Mount in it and therefore the power manifested
> was Christian. Pentecost divorced from the
> Sermon on the Mount is spiritual pow-wow
> instead of spiritual power.

Jones had also written that a group "asked ourselves
whether in Christ we had a message that was vital and
inescapable if we were to find life and God," and he
replied "We were driven at once to the Sermon on the
Mount" (Jones, *The Christ of the Mount, supra*, p. 7).
He suggested a creed that says, "I believe in the
Sermon on the Mount and in its way of life, and I
intend, God helping me, to embody it" (p. 12). He
added: "The greatest need of modern Christianity is the
rediscovery of the Sermon on the Mount as the only
practical way to live" (p. 14)

Put the statements of Chambers side by side. Note that
Chambers points to power (from the faith of Jesus
Christ) as necessary to a life lived by the Sermon. Jones
points to the Sermon as the very content of the power
of Christian faith. And if we look at James, Corinthians,
and the Sermon together, we can learn rather quickly
that the early A.A. pioneers were looking at both
pictures. They insisted on a new birth. Then studied
how to implement their "new man nature" in "doing"
God's will.

Neither the teachings of Jesus in the Sermon nor of Paul
in Corinthians nor of James in the Book of James is to
be examined in a vacuum or as a mere reiteration of

Old Testament Law. All teach and promote a new gospel—a new creation, a new man in Christ that not only teaches the will of God, but brings the power of God into a believer's life, transforming his nature and enabling him to manifest God's power and love in his very way of life.

Evidence as to Author and Date of the Book of James

Though still an issue, there are many who believe that James, the Lord's brother, is probably the author of the Book of James*: The New Bible Dictionary* (*supra*) contains a thoughtful discussion of the still existing questions about the authorship of the Book of James. In brief form, so does *The Companion Bible*, where the scholar E. Bullinger wrote: "The Epistle of James has been the subject of controversy both as regards the identity of the writer, and as to the time of writing" (p. 1847, note 3). This question of identity is: Was the author James, the Lord's brother, or was that author James someone else? There has been uncertainty about the authorship, and there have been several theories that attempt to resolve the question. For these and other reasons, the Epistle of James did not receive general acceptance in the West until the 4th Century. But *The New Bible Dictionary* concludes as follows: "It seems logical to suppose that either James himself composed the Word, or else a secretary or later redactor compiled it from James's sermons." See *New Bible Dictionary*, pp. 550-551. The eminent Bible scholar Bullinger is more emphatic: "There is little doubt, however, that the writer was James, 'the Lord's brother'." (*The Companion Bible*, *supra*, p. 1847, n.1).

The Date of Writing and the Contention that the Epistle of James was the First Written of the New Testament Documents: It is fair to say that the dating of Biblical manuscripts is hardly an exact science and involves many approaches and differing views among those who attempt it. While there are differing views on the date the epistle James was written (some arguing for A.D. 67 and some for A.D. 45), the scholar Bullinger quotes the highly regarded Bishop Lightfoot as follows: "And a careful study of the chronological question has convinced me that they are right who hold the Epistle of James to be perhaps the earliest of the New Testament writings. It belongs to that period of the Pentecostal dispensation when the whole Church was Jewish, and when their meeting-places still bore the Jewish designation of 'synagogues'." (*The Companion Bible, supra*, p.1847, note 3). Then, in Appendix 180, at page 208, Bullinger lays out the chronology of the Acts period and following, showing the Epistle of James as occurring during the days of Claudius, and having been written in 45 A.D.

Concluding Thoughts about the Book of James and James Its Author

The Book of James was accepted as canon in 367, 393, and 397 A.D. (Megivern, *Bible Interpretation, supra*, p.37, 48, 66). It well may be the first written of the canonical books of the New Testament (Schaff, *History of the Christian Church, Volume I, supra*, p. 270). James, the Lord's brother, probably wrote it or promulgated its contents. Consistent with his alleged pre-eminence in the Jewish church, the probable author James begins James 1:1 by stating: "James, a servant of God and of the Lord Jesus Christ, to the twelve tribes which are scattered abroad, greeting."

Though James was not one of the twelve, he did command special respect and have special stature at a later point as the brother of Jesus and as an apparent pillar of the Jewish Christian church at Jerusalem (See Schaff, *History, supra*, pp. 339-350; Harnack, *The Expansion of Christianity, Vol. I, supra*, p. 92). In fact, as the other Apostles seemed to vanish from Biblical accounts, there remains frequent mention of three leaders: Peter, Paul, and James, the Lord's brother. And I believe that, although we still just don't know exactly who wrote the Book of James or when it was written, we can state that it has been an accepted part of the New Testament for many centuries now and is consistent with the other Christian works.

End

Appendix 5

The Difference an Identification of the Creator Makes

Early A.A. pioneers in Akron had no lack of understanding and no doubt as to the identity of the Creator on Whom they were placing their reliance and no doubt as to the identity of His son Jesus Christ who provided the way to establishing their relationship with Him.

The confused state of idolatry, nonsense gods, and fabricated names for some nebulous "power" in A.A. and 12 Step groups can be readily dissolved with some solid history of early A.A. But continuing with the foolishness simply means that A.A. and other Twelve Step fellowships have the heart carved out of their Steps and the hole replaced with the formula: "Don't drink, and go to meetings." The resultant poor success rates of today can be arrested, and they should be.

A.A.'s Basic Text Speaks Very Clearly about Almighty God--the Creator

According to recent counts, the word "God"—considered together with pronouns and other Biblical descriptions referring to Him--is used more than 400 times in each of the several editions of A.A.'s Big Book.

Also, both A.A.'s Big Book and the writings of its founders make clear that the God of the Bible is the reference intended. Thus the following words are used in the Big Book of Almighty God: the Creator, Maker,

God, Almighty God, Father of light, Father, Heavenly Father, Lord, God of our fathers, Spirit, and others. These descriptive words are plain and well understood from the King James Version of the Bible that early AAs used and studied.

The Intrusions of New Thought, New Age, and Nonsense gods

Before A.A. began, New Thought writers were speaking of a "higher power." That strange phrase is found in the writings of Ralph Waldo Trine and Professor William James, Emmanuel Movement writings, and the language of Emmet Fox. It coincides with the substitutionary language so characteristic of New Age thinking as well. Thus the Biblical word "God" is given a new and different meaning; "Christ" is given a new and different meaning; and, similarly, other Biblical words are assigned new meanings.

The Bible Used by Early AAs Contained Some Simple Guides and Admonitions

In the beginning, God (Hebrew: *elohim*): The power and work of the Creator are described in the very first verse of the Bible: "In the beginning, God created the heaven and the earth" (Genesis 1:1). The English word "God" in verse one is the translation of the Hebrew word *elohim* in the Hebrew text underlying the King James Version. Some Bible versions have chosen to transliterate the Hebrew word *elohim* into English rather than translate it as "God." For example, *The Hebraic-Roots Version Scriptures* translates Genesis 1:1

as follows: "In the beginning Elohim created the heaven and the earth" [James Scott Trimm. *The Hebraic-Roots Version Scriptures*. (Texas: The Society for the Advancement of Nazarene Judaism, 2004), p. 5]. The Hebrew word *elohim* is commonly translated as "God" in most of its occurrences in the King James Version (and in most other Bible versions as well). [See Wigram, *The New Englishman's Hebrew/Aramaic Concordance to the Old Testament*. (____: Christian Copyrights, Inc., 1983), pp. 79-93].

God plainly declared that His own personal name was and is the Hebrew word *hwhy* (usually written "YHWH", and represented and pronounced as "Yahweh" in English). In the King James Version, the Hebrew text of Exodus 3:15 is translated as follows: "And God said moreover unto Moses, Thus shalt thou say unto the children of Israel, The LORD God of your fathers, the God of Abraham, the God of Isaac, and the God of Jacob, hath sent me unto you: this is my name forever, and this is my memorial unto all generations." *The Hebraic-Roots Version Scriptures* transliterates *elohim* ("God") and YHWH ("Yahweh") in Exodus 3:15, and translates the verse as follows: "And Elohim said unto Moshe [Moses]: Thus shall you say unto the children of Yisra'el: YHWH, the Elohim of your fathers, the Elohim of Avraham, the Elohim of Yitzchak, and the Elohim of Yaakov, has sent me unto you; this *is MY name for ever, and this is my memorial unto all generations."* In this version, it is clearer in the English translation that the Creator Himself declares that His proper name is "YHWH" ("Yahweh").

In the King James Version, the Hebrew text of Exodus 6:3 is translated as follows: "I appeared unto Abraham, unto Isaac, and unto Jacob by *the name of* God Almighty, but by my name JEHOVAH was I not known unto them." *The Hebraic-Roots Version Scriptures* transliterates the Hebrew words *el* (translated "God" in most Bible versions), *shaddai* ("Almighty"), and YHWH ("Yahweh"), and translates the verse as follows: "And I appeared unto Avraham, unto Yitzchak, and unto Yaakov, in El Shaddai, and by My name YHWH was I not known to them?" Again in this version, it is clearer in the English translation that the Creator Himself declares that His proper name is "YHWH" ("Yahweh").

God's personal name, YHWH ("Yahweh"), is used more than 6,800 times in the Hebrew text underlying the King James Version (and other major Bible versions). Recently, I traveled to Mobile, Alabama, to see an exhibition of a the largest number of biblical Dead Sea Scrolls ever put on display outside of the Bible lands. The manuscripts dated approximately from between 200 B.C. to 50 A.D. In the Psalms scroll, I saw that the Creator's proper name was faithfully preserved and written in the Paleo-Hebrew script, even though the more recent Hebrew square script was used for every other word in the scroll.

God sought to protect and be praised for that personal name: He commanded:

1. "Thou shalt have no other gods before Me" (Exodus 20:3).
2. "You shall not take the name of YHWH your Elohim in vain; for YHWH will not hold him guiltless that takes His name in vain" (Exodus 20:7).

3. "I will give thanks unto YHWH according to His righteousness; and will sing praise to the name of YHWH Elyon" (Psalm 7:18).
4. "O YHWH, our Adon, how glorious is Your name in all the earth . . ." (Psalm 8:1).
5. "And blessed be His glorious name for ever . . ." (Psalm 72:19).
6. "Let them praise Your name as great and awful . . ." (Psalm 99:3).

The nonsense "higher power" and similar language today with its absurd names for "a god" or for some "Force" outside ourselves is both confusing and an affront to our Creator, in addition to being just plain idol worship. Or, more simply expressed, it is just plain "idle" worship—useless to the nth degree

It's hard to understand and believe that intelligent people writing official A.A. publications today, and sending out letters on A.A. stationary, frequently tell the reader that some AAs call "their" power God; that some call "it" the group; that some believe in "something"; and that some believe in nothing at all. And perhaps truer words were never spoken when it comes to describing the polyglot crowds that pour into the doors of A.A. today. But the publications and the writers are supposed to be talking about a "recovery" program--not a nonsense kindergarten. To prove the point, you need only refer to A.A.'s Big Book (which is called its "basic text") to see what even today's recovery program calls for. The text says quite plainly: "There is One who has all power. That One is God. May you find Him now." That God—*Elohim*—our Creator— has only one personal name—YAHWEH. The reference is

not to a "group" or "something" or "nothing at all." To
suggest otherwise is wrong. Yet every day in A.A.
brings forth some new absurd name for a "god."
Frequently, there are statements in the fellowship and
in its writings that "god" can be a tree, a chair, a rock,
a radiator, a light bulb, a goddess, a rainbow, the Big
Dipper, Santa Claus, the rear end of a bus, Gertrude,
Ralph, "Him, Her, or It," Something, Someone, not-god
(whoever that might be other than the Devil himself),
or nothing at all.

Worship or praise or prayer or giving thanks to, or
asking forgiveness or blessing or healing from, a chair,
a light bulb, a "not-god," or nothing at all is ridiculous.
It assumes we are all dummies. It blows (in fact blasts)
a wind of foolishness in the face of sick, bewildered,
helpless new people. If offers nothing that a reputable
professional should put his name to. Certainly not a
purported scholar, academic, or scientist. It is not
grounded in early A.A. It occupies no place in the
beliefs of Roman Catholics, Protestants, or Jews. And if
there are those who buy this wild jargon, I am with Dr.
Bob's statement about atheists and agnostics and
skeptics: "I feel sorry for you" (Big Book, p. 181). A
salute to a goofy god is idolatry. It is useless and
pointless. And it is an insult to the Creator, God
Almighty, whose personal name is Yahweh.
Furthermore, if and when we call Him by His declared
name, we wouldn't give a fig for those who associate
some assumed "god" with a chair, Gertrude, or a
radiator. Nor would we question that He, Yahweh, is the
one to whom Bill Wilson referred when he spoke of "the
God of our fathers" and of the "Father of Light." If A.A.
is no longer a religion, as a few still like to say, then
why in the world would it continue to manufacture gods

that have more relationship to a Detroit auto factory than to the healing ministry that went on when early AAs were being cured. Either radiators cure, or they don't. And since they don't, let's give the Creator, Yahweh, the credit and praise He deserves.

END

About the Author

Dick B. writes books on the spiritual roots of Alcoholics Anonymous. They show how the basic and highly successful biblical ideas used by early AAs can be valuable tools for success in today's A.A. His research can also help the religious and recovery communities work more effectively with alcoholics, addicts, and others involved in Twelve Step programs.

The author is an active, recovered member of A.A.; a retired attorney; and a Bible student. He has sponsored more than one hundred men in their recovery from alcoholism. Consistent with A.A.'s traditions of anonymity, he uses the pseudonym "Dick B."

He has had twenty-eight titles published including: *Dr. Bob and His Library*; *Anne Smith's Journal, 1933-1939*; *The Oxford Group & Alcoholics Anonymous*; *The Akron Genesis of Alcoholics Anonymous*; *The Books Early AAs Read for Spiritual Growth*; *New Light on Alcoholism: God, Sam Shoemaker, and A.A.*; *Courage to Change* (with Bill Pittman); *Cured: Proven Help for Alcoholics and Addicts; The Good Book and The Big Book: A.A.'s Roots in the Bible*; *That Amazing Grace: The Role of Clarence and Grace S. in Alcoholics Anonymous*; *Good Morning!: Quiet Time, Morning Watch, Meditation, and Early A.A.*; *Turning Point: A History of Early A.A.'s Spiritual Roots and Successes, Hope!: The Story of Geraldine D., Alina Lodge & Recovery; Utilizing Early A.A.'s Spiritual Roots for Recovery Today; The Golden Text of A.A.; By the Power of God; God and Alcoholism; Making Known the Biblical History of A.A.; Why Early A.A. Succeeded*; *Comments of Dick B. at The First Nationwide A.A. History Conference; Henrietta Seiberling: Ohio's Lady with a Cause; and The James Club*. The books have been the subject of newspaper articles and reviews in *Library Journal, Bookstore Journal, The Living Church, Faith at Work, Sober Times, Episcopal Life, Recovery News, Ohioana Quarterly, The PHOENIX*, and *The Saint Louis University Theology Digest*. They are listed in the biographies of major addiction center, religion, and religious history sites. He has published over 150 articles on his subject, most posted on the internet.

Dick is the father of two sons (Ken and Don) and has two granddaughters. As a young man, he did a stint as a newspaper reporter. He attended the University of California, Berkeley, where he received his A.A. degree with Honorable Mention, majored in economics, and was elected to Phi Beta Kappa in his Junior year. In the United States Army, he was an Information-Education Specialist. He received his A.B. and J.D. degrees from Stanford University, and was Case Editor of the Stanford Law Review. Dick became interested in Bible study in his childhood Sunday School and was much inspired by his mother's almost daily study of Scripture. He joined, and was president of, a Community Church affiliated with the United Church of Christ. By 1972, he was studying the origins of the Bible and began traveling abroad in pursuit of that subject. In 1979, he became much involved in a Biblical research, teaching, and fellowship ministry. In his community life, he was president of a merchants' council, Chamber of Commerce, church retirement center, and homeowners' association. He served on a public district board and has held offices in a service club.

In 1986, he was felled by alcoholism, gave up his law practice, and began recovery as a member of the Fellowship of Alcoholics Anonymous. In 1990, his interest in A.A.'s Biblical/Christian roots was sparked by his attendance at A.A.'s International Convention in Seattle. He has traveled widely; researched at archives, and at public and seminary libraries; interviewed scholars, historians, clergy, A.A. "old-timers" and survivors; and participated in programs and conferences on A.A.'s roots.

The author is the owner of Good Book Publishing Company and has several works in progress. Much of his research and writing is done in collaboration with his older son, Ken, an ordained minister, who holds B.A., B.Th., and M.A. degrees. Ken has been a lecturer in New Testament Greek at a Bible college and a lecturer in Fundamentals of Oral Communication at San Francisco State University. Ken is a computer specialist and director of marketing and research in Hawaii ethanol projects.

Dick is a member of the American Historical Association, Research Society on Alcoholism, Alcohol and Drugs History Society, Organization of American Historians, The Association for Medical Education and Research in Substance Abuse, Coalition of Prison Evangelists, Christian Association for Psychological Studies, and International Substance Abuse and Addictions Coalition. He is available for conferences, panels, seminars, and interviews.

Good Book Publishing Company Order Form

(Use this form to order Dick B.'s titles on early A.A.'s roots and successes)

Qty.	Titles by Dick B.	Price	
____	*A New Way In*	$19.95 ea. $	_____
____	*A New Way Out*	$19.95 ea. $	_____
____	*Anne Smith's Journal, 1933-1939*	$22.95 ea. $	_____
____	*By the Power of God: A Guide to Early A.A. Groups and Forming Similar Groups Today*	$23.95 ea. $	_____
____	*Cured! Proven Help for Alcoholics and Addicts*	$23.95 ea. $	_____
____	*Dr. Bob and His Library*	$22.95 ea. $	_____
____	*Dr. Bob of Alcoholics Anonymous*	$24.95 ea. $	_____
____	*God and Alcoholism*	$21.95 ea. $	_____
____	*Good Morning! Quiet Time, Morning Watch, Meditation, and Early A.A.*	$22.95 ea. $	_____
____	*Henrietta B. Seiberling*	$20.95 ea. $	_____
____	*Introduction to the Sources and Founding of A.A.*	$22.95 ea. $	_____
____	*Making Known the Biblical History and Roots of Alcoholics Anonymous*	$24.95 ea. $	_____
____	*New Light on Alcoholism: God, Sam Shoemaker, and A.A.*	$24.95 ea. $	_____
____	*Real Twelve Step Fellowship History*	$23.95 ea. $	_____
____	*That Amazing Grace: The Role of Clarence and Grace S. in Alcoholics Anonymous*	$22.95 ea. $	_____
____	*The Akron Genesis of Alcoholics Anonymous*	$23.95 ea. $	_____
____	*The Books Early AAs Read for Spiritual Growth*	$21.95 ea. $	_____
____	*The Conversion of Bill W.*	$23.95 ea. $	_____
____	*The First Nationwide A.A. History Conference*	$22.95 ea. $	_____
____	*The Golden Text of A.A.*	$20.95 ea. $	_____
____	*The Good Book and the Big Book: A.A.'s Roots in the Bible*	$23.95 ea. $	_____
____	*The Good Book-Big Book Guidebook*	$22.95 ea. $	_____
____	*The James Club and the Original A.A. Program's Absolute Essentials*	$23.95 ea. $	_____
____	*The Oxford Group and Alcoholics Anonymous*	$23.95 ea. $	_____
____	*Turning Point: A History of Early A.A.'s Spiritual Roots and Successes*	$29.95 ea. $	_____
____	*Twelve Steps for You*	$21.95 ea. $	_____
____	*Utilizing Early A.A.'s Spiritual Roots for Recovery Today*	$20.95 ea. $	_____
____	*When Early AAs Were Cured and Why*	$23.95 ea. $	_____
____	*Why Early A.A. Succeeded*	$23.95 ea. $	_____

(Order Form continued on the next page)

Good Book Publishing Company Order Form
(continued from the previous page)

Order Subtotal: $ _____

Shipping and Handling (S&H) **: $ _____

(** For Shipping and Handling, please add 10% of the Order Subtotal for U.S. orders or 15% of the Order Subtotal for international orders. The minimum U.S. S&H is $5.60. The minimum S&H for Canada and Mexico is US$ 9.95. The minimum S&H for other countries is US$ 11.95.)

Order Total: $ _____

Credit card: VISA   MasterCard   American Express   Discover   (circle one)

Account number: _____ Exp.: _____

Name: _____ (as it is on your credit card, if using one)

(Company: _____)

Address Line 1: _____

Address Line 2: _____

City: _____ State/Prov.: _____

Zip/Postal Code: _____ Country: _____

Signature: _____ Telephone: _____

Email: _____

No returns accepted. Please mail this Order Form, along with your check or money order (if sending one), to: Dick B., c/o Good Book Publishing Company, PO Box 837, Kihei, HI 96753-0837. Please make your check or money order (if sending one) payable to "Dick B." in U.S. dollars drawn on a U.S. bank. If you have any questions, please phone: 1-808-874-4876 or send an email message to: dickb@dickb.com. Dick B.'s web site: www.DickB.com.

If you would like to purchase Dick B.'s entire 29-volume reference set on early A.A.'s roots and successes (and how those successes may be replicated today) at a substantial discount, please send Dick B. an email message or give him a call.

Paradise Research Publications, Inc.
PO Box 837
Kihei, HI 96753-0837
(808) 874-4876
Email: dickb@dickb.com
URL: http://www.dickb.com/index.shtml
http://www.dickb-blog.com

Made in the USA
Lexington, KY
15 September 2012